JFK, Jr.,
AND ME

JFK, Jr., AND ME

The Other Side of Camelot

ROBERT CHARTUK

JFK, Jr., AND ME
The Other Side of Camelot

iUniverse books may be ordered through booksellers or by contacting:

iUniverse
1663 Liberty Drive
Bloomington, IN 47403
www.iuniverse.com
1-800-Authors (1-800-288-4677)

ISBN: 978-1-4917-6373-5 (sc)
ISBN: 978-1-4917-6374-2 (e)

Library of Congress Control Number: 2015904297

Print information available on the last page.

iUniverse rev. date: 06/02/2015

INTRODUCTION

Yes, to answer your question, I was obsessed with John F. Kennedy, Jr., and jealous too. Who wouldn't be? Born a month apart, our life trajectories couldn't have been more different, yet our paths tragically crossed. His star lit the universe while I lurked in the shadows; he flourished at the pinnacle of fame and fortune and I dwelled at the bottom dreaming, pretending, and then left shattered by the loss of my idol.

The barflies want me to tell the story, to make some sense of it. But who am I? I can't pretend to know why God lets some live and others die; how some have it all while others, who deserve nothing, take it from them.

If I'm going to tell it, I'm going to tell everything. If you're squeamish and have yet to come to terms with life and death and fate, stop reading. If you want to drink it in and watch perplexed as I am, please continue, and perhaps, when you're done, explain it to me.

BOOK I:
THE END

CHAPTER 1

CONFIRMATION

Waves pitched the patrol boat and my stomach heaved with it. We were next to a huge Navy ship, its crane reaching over the water like a giant claw. All eyes focused on a cable disappearing below and then the colors appeared, red, blue, and white. A twisted mass that was an airplane hung vibrant against the North Atlantic's pale blue water.

It was the wreckage of John F. Kennedy, Jr., son of our 33rd President, scion of Camelot, the most intriguing man of my generation. Gone with him was his wife, Carolyn, and her sister, Lauren Bessette, their great destinies snuffed just a few miles short of Martha's Vineyard.

The crew set down the mangled craft like a sleeping baby. On deck were Senator Edward Kennedy, John's uncle, and Congressman Patrick Kennedy, his cousin. Their confirmation was certain. It was the end.

CHAPTER 2

THE TALKER

"It's nine o'clock on a Saturday, regular crowd shuffles in," the Piano Man sings from the jukebox, and here I am, sipping away my troubles at my hometown bar. I stare at the scrapes left by the barstools in the floor.

"What's ailing you, Mr. Doom and Gloom?" asks The Talker, eyes squinting from the smoke of his cigarette. The Talker sits at the core of the cocktail universe, buying drinks and entertaining the troops. The girls in his orbit giggle.

The answer appears on the TV's hung in every corner: John F. Kennedy, Jr. is dead, his plane pulled from the water off Massachusetts.

"Just not too friendly tonight, that's all."

The bar tunes back to the non-stop John John.

A flag-draped coffin proceeds down Pennsylvania Avenue atop a carriage pulled by a team of horses. A small boy, dressed in powder blue, snaps to attention and salutes.

"Who's up for another drink?" The Talker trolls for his crowd back, but cannot compete with the tragedy. Gracing the screen is Carolyn, blond hair flowing, peeved by the throng camped outside her door. Paparazzi angle for the money shot, reporters grope for a tidbit. The gallant John pleads for just a little peace.

The room takes a drink. The heir is gone.

"What a shame," says The Talker. "I'm glad I'm not him."

"You'd love to be him," I shoot back, startled by my liquid courage. "We all wanted to be him."

"What the hell's that supposed to mean?" The Talker parries, backed by his posse.

"I wanted to be like him. I'm not denying it. And I bet you did too."

The crowd felt the challenge. "You're just a jealous piece of shit," he chirped. "I have my own life. I don't have to be like someone else to be happy."

The bartender intervenes, his ear tuned to such trouble. "Who's up," he calls to the barflies. "Next one's on me."

The Talker waves him off, eyes still glaring.

"I was right there," I stammer. "I was there when they found him."

"The hell you were."

CHAPTER 3

TAKING FLIGHT

A few years before, I was drawn to an airport in Westhampton, on Eastern Long Island, to chase my own dream to fly. I drove there with a blend of exhilaration and terror in my gut and found that the address of the Sky Sailor's Glider School, Rust Avenue, did little to ease my fear. But I had Dramamine in my pocket and some money to burn, so I signed up to soar!

My instructor's idea of a lesson was to give you the stick and let you figure it out for yourself. I named him Gruff. Gliders are as basic a flying machine as you can get and the frailty of the craft is the first thing that strikes you. In the world of aviation, lighter is better and I wondered if the plane's paper-thin skin would hold up for just one more flight. "Looks good," said Gruff, slapping his hand on the wing. "Get in."

The glider owes a lion's share of its success to the tow plane needed to take it aloft. At the other end of a long line was a single engine contraption that had seen better days, as did its pilot, the operator of the Sky Sailor's school, also named John, whose only words of advice amounted to: "Whatever you do, don't pull my tail up."

Gruff strapped me in, climbed into the rear seat and shoved a bulky set of earphones onto my head. His presence at the other set of controls was the only iota of comfort I could grasp as the line snapped taut and started us moving.

"Hand on the stick, feet on the pedals," Gruff commanded.

A tiny wheel at the end of the wing allowed the plane, tilted to one side like a wounded bird, to roll along. I could feel Gruff's hand wiggle the controls and then, finding the center, let them rest in my trembling hands. It didn't take much speed for the wings to bite enough air to level the glider and in no time we were hurtling down the runway straight and nice.

With a belch of smoke, the tow plane lurched skyward. Being a newly-minted member of the "just-get-in-and-fly" glider program, I had only a vague idea of what to do next. So I yanked the stick toward me and felt the glider jump off the runway. My glee was short lived as Gruff's hand fought back. I was taking us too high too fast and instantly divined the meaning of the tow pilot's last words. Had I continued my abrupt path skyward, I would have pulled his tail up and driven his nose straight into the ground.

Good save, Gruff!

The sun sparkled off the ocean ahead of us and I spotted the small, white cottage where I was staying for the summer.

Could Gruff feel my legs shaking through the pedals?

"Okay," John crackled over the headset.

"Pull the lever," yelled Gruff.

My eyes darted around the cockpit.

"The red handle, to the left."

My hand trembled toward it.

"Pull!"

A jolt set us free and John flared hard left. Gruff banked us right.

I was struck by the utter silence of it all. There was no noise, not even a feeling of movement as we soared across the sky. It felt like we were in a tiny box balanced on the head of a pin 3,000 feet in the air.

"It's all yours," Gruff said from behind.

So this is what it's like to be free!

I had been stuck at sea level for far too long and finally, it was my time to fly!

With the trepidation of a bomb diffuser, I tilted the stick ever so slightly to the right. The glider lurched in that direction and I could feel my right pedal get pushed toward the floor.

"Put some pedal into it when you turn," Gruff called out.

Stick and pedal together is a beautiful thing and the glider banked into a long, smooth turn. I nudged the stick toward the left and gingerly applied the pedal. The plane made a majestic arc back the other way. I was flying! To the right again, this time a little sharper, and to the left. I was amazed how this frail machine responded as I zigzagged my way across the sky.

"Let's try this," Gruff said, pushing the stick forward and plunging us straight down. The white cottage raced toward me and I pondered the irony of crashing into my own place of residence. As my life passed before me, Gruff fought the stick all the way back, pulling the plane out of its dive and back up into the sky. I pushed the stick forward to level off, but Gruff held firm. With the momentum built up from its great plunge, the plane climbed straight up and then upside down and then into the backside of a complete loop! My stomach, now somewhere near my neck, was dueling with my brain for oxygen. Arcing back down from the loop was the fastest I ever travelled. At the bottom, Gruff let the stick find its center and the plane leveled with a nonchalance that left me gasping.

That night, in the delicate space between consciousness and sleep, thoughts of cheating death and returning safely to earth put my life into a glorious, new perspective. I know John John felt the same.

Chapter 4

MY HOME TOWN

My home town of Center Moriches is not the epicenter of anything. This seaside community, a quick seagull flight across Moriches Bay from the Atlantic Ocean, was boring and its young captives were left to create their own diversions. We didn't realize it growing up, but our town was a little Eden with desolate, white beaches, fish, crabs, and clams in every cove, and the ocean so close you could smell it at night. We were near enough to the vibrant New York City to feel its shadow, but we felt isolated, never allowing ourselves to dream.

We played in the water, hated school, and hung out in cliques, preoccupied with the drama of teenage relationships. Whatever we did, wherever we went, there was nothing we didn't highlight with a wash of beer and a puff of smoke.

Then some Sunshine came to town. A fellow named Stretch pedaled his bike from Westhampton and brought with him a sandwich bag of LSD. Everyone in their teenage years got a hold of it and four in the morning was a carnival with kids skipping through the streets, marveling at the stars and the moon and each other. It was a cruel taste of what their world could be, of colors and insight and fantastic opportunity. Woodstock had sparked a new age of enlightenment not too many years before, but the elation ran out when Stretch disappeared and everyone was deported back to their hopeless existence.

The casualties were immediate. One kid downed too many of the little tabs and we saw him raving at the night as we rolled by on our bikes, the path ahead pulsating like the Yellow Brick Road. He killed himself a short time later. Another kid, unlucky to have money to buy a lot of it, kept the fantasy alive too long. After a few years of struggle, he too, took his life.

The carefree days of youth drained from my soul, I took refuge at the Sports Page Bar and Restaurant, a place where I could drink and slink back to the comfort of my fellow underachievers. I was traveling a lot in the wake of the Kennedy crash in my job as a public relations man for the government and I was depressed and being here was the only relief I could fathom. Like everyone else, I didn't have a drinking problem and could get back on the wagon anytime I wanted, but I wasn't on it at the moment and had to subsist with life at the bar.

My mind flips through a book called the *Illustrated History of the Moriches Bay Area.* Here's a picture of the bar when it was the Long Island Hotel a hundred years ago. And here's my house on Main Street, the 1918 Taft House next to the funeral home, and next to that, the school where I went from K through 12. When I die, I tell people, just wheel me over to the funeral home and I will have completed my entire life cycle in one place like a salmon. At the other end of town is the little ginger bread house where I grew up, a place where my mother still lives. Gone is the huge building at Carr's Block, decrepit after all its years. This was where my dentist, Dr. Hirsch, traumatized my youth with his ancient drill. I still remember the strings laboring across the pulleys which drove the drill too slow to do the job without great pain. I cringe from the time the suction tube backfired and filled my mouth with spittle. I swig my drink and slush it around like the Lavoris mouthwash offered by Dr. Hirsch in a pointy little cup. I'll never forgive the weasel barber next door who took all the coins my mother gave me for a haircut and some candy afterward. I was there when a wrecking ball crashed the remains of the Carr Block to the ground, the residents shaking their heads as the landmark fell.

I'm sitting in the seat where Jerry Duffy, my childhood friend, sat for the last time. He didn't go to Center Moriches High School like the rest of us. He went to the Catholic school, Mercy High, where they had a football team. He excelled on the gridiron and there were high hopes he would break through to the big time.

That night, Jerry became more obnoxious with every drink. None of us had the gumption to tell him to shut up already, though we were all thinking it. But there was a stranger at the bar who, hearing enough, finally mouthed our sentiments: "Why don't you shut the fuck up?"

The assault on Duffy's manhood would not go unchallenged and after some bold threats, the conversation moved out the back door. This was the last we would hear from Jerry Duffy. The stranger broke his neck and ended his dreams with a single punch.

The Long Island Hotel was the bar of my father and of his. It was a place where you could down a few before going home to face the family. It was the place where my friend Harvard celebrated his birthday with the bold initiative of downing a shot of whiskey for each of his 18 years. Just as his twelfth glass joined the others in a crooked line down the bar, his father showed up and dragged him outside in a headlock. He karate chopped his noggin a few times, all the while cussing up a blue streak, and then, to everyone's amazement, let him go back inside. With his father's love expressed in a few lumps on his head, Harvard was back in business. The crowd chanting his name and the proprietor grinning, Harvard slammed down his 18th glass. The Talker raised up his arm in victory. Harvard absorbed the accolades for a moment and then wobbled out to his Galaxy 500 parked out front. He fired it up and proceeded to screech out the nastiest burnout Main Street would ever know. He rigged his car so just the front brakes would lock and the back tires, free to spin, billowed the downtown with acrid smoke.

Eyes wild and gritting his teeth like a madman, the birthday boy would have burned the tires to the rims had he not encountered the second father figure of his evening. Creeping through the haze like a black cat came Harry the Cop who stopped his cruiser behind Harvard's fire-belching dragon. The birthday boy didn't see him at first and kept the engine roaring. But his expression quickly deflated when Harry flipped on his siren and his cherry top ricocheted red light through the clouds.

"Let him go. Let him go," the crowd chanted. One of us informed the cop it was Harvard's birthday and, to our renewed amazement, let him off with just a warning.

CHAPTER 5

FLIGHT 800

"So you were flying airplanes, too?" The Talker sarcastically asked one slow night. "That makes you an expert on what happened to John Kennedy?"

"No, but I know what he went through."

"Oh really," The Talker dripped. "Why don't you tell us all about it?"

"Well, if it wasn't for the Flight 800 crash, I wouldn't even have been out there."

"Out where?" Harvard cut in.

"On the boat, when they found Kennedy."

The bar was empty and I was a little loaded, so I laid the story on thicker and heavier as I went:

I was shut in at a tiny beach house overlooking Moriches Bay. When I say shut in, I mean sealed up inside on account of the most ornery mosquito population ever conjured by the diabolical Gods that torture men. These were the dreaded salt marsh mosquito, which have been known to chase people down the beach like angry bees. After shutting the windows and sealing up the air conditioner with all matters of tape and Styrofoam, I was still bedeviled by an endless barrage of the little vampires. I put towels under the doors and wadded tissue paper in the window jambs, all the while smashing their gory little bodies, some with drops of my precious blood, into minute works of art onto the white cottage walls. A particularly aggressive buzzer caught my eye and I was able to trace his path from his point of entry to my neck.

They were coming in from the heating ducts! After taping off the grills, I settled into my seclusion which was a shame since the little house, mere feet from the bay, afforded a panoramic water view.

A little after sundown, the phone rang. It was my boss with the National Oceanic and Atmospheric Administration, the bureaucratic parent of the National Weather Service where I worked, calling from Washington.

"What's going on out there, Bob?"

"I don't know."

"There was a plane crash. I think somewhere near you."

"Lemme go outside and take a look."

Exiting into the steamy night air, I was confronted by a scene from a disaster movie.

"Holy smokes," I told him. "The sky's all lit up and there's helicopters and planes all over the place." A police boat sped across the bay. "Looks like something really bad happened."

"It was an airliner, a TWA flight," said my boss. "It's on the news."

White flares illuminated the sky and the horizon pulsed with an eerie orange glow. I heard the drone of engines and one after the other, a boat or aircraft would scream by. I took in the scene as long as I could before the mosquito search party drove me back inside.

TWA Flight 800 heading for Paris crashed in a great fireball into the Atlantic Ocean shortly after takeoff from John F. Kennedy International Airport.

The phone jarred me awake the next morning, my boss again.

"Bob, NOAA has a ship on its way to the crash site. Its specialty is locating obstructions in harbors and channels to create maps for navigation. They're going to use it to find the plane. I'm making arrangements for you to take a news crew from ABC out there to meet the ship. It'll be a great opportunity to get NOAA in the headlines."

"I'm on it."

I was to meet a local charter boat captain to take me and the crew out to rendezvous with our ship. I was a little hungry and on my way to the dock, I made a bad choice. Instead of the drug store for seasick pills, I went to Carvel for a large black raspberry shake.

I had never met Captain Wayne, but he recognized me. Our fathers were friends a long time ago during World War II and it turns out, my Dad was the captain's godfather. His boat, built for sport fishing, had a nice cruising speed and we quickly passed through Moriches Inlet into the ocean. Having a small boat on the bay for a few years myself, I was familiar with our course. In fact, I was out there the day before and wondered what I would have done if I was there when the plane went down.

Captain Wayne hailed the NOAA ship Rude (pronounced Rudy) on the radio and speeding toward it we saw the lights of the many different boats now engaged not in search and rescue, but in recovery. Hope for anyone surviving such a fall from the sky was gone.

"Area off limits! What's your business here?" yelled a sailor from a Coast Guard boat that appeared suddenly out of the setting sun, his arm cocked as if he was itching to draw his pistol. Everyone looked at me.

"We're with NOAA," I shouted across the gap. "That's our ship the Rude. We're meeting up with it." The cameraman filmed the encounter.

"Turn off the camera, sir," the officer barked, his hand closing in on the gun. He scowled until the cameraman finished jamming the equipment back into its case.

"Stand by," he ordered as he turned to squawk into his radio.

"You have no clearance," he shot back. "Please leave the area immediately."

"I have orders from Washington. Your headquarters should clear us."

He barked back into his radio.

"Headquarters has no knowledge. I need you to leave now."

The newsmen were crestfallen. They knew they were the only reporters on the scene and were anticipating a major scoop.

"Have them call my supervisor," I yelled back, annunciating the phone number. "His name is Tim Tomastik."

"Stand by."

Minutes passed with the boat rising up and down like a pendulum in slow motion. Scorched pieces of foam and fabric floated by and the sticky smell of jet fuel hung in the air. My stomach churned.

"You're clear," our captor finally came back, not much friendlier. "Proceed with caution."

CHAPTER 6

BIG DADDY

Another lazy evening saw the usuals mope into the watering hole, one of whom was a grizzled-looking cat we called Big Daddy. "I was there for the bodies," he said to no one in particular. "We were out fishing and right around sunset, saw the whole thing. There was a streak of light like a missile heading up into the sky and then the explosion. There was no sound at first, and then it hit us square in the chest. By then the pieces were falling down in streaks of flames and smoke. We took off after it."

The Talker hailed Big Daddy like a hero. "Now here's a guy who was right in the middle of it," he said in my direction. "You were pulling in the bodies, weren't you Daddy?"

"It was about nine miles out and when we got there the ocean was on fire from the jet fuel. I was blinded by the smoke and had to find my way through the flames, but I got us into an area where everything was floating. My boat's meant for the canyon and has halogens for night fishing. It was weird—wherever the light hit, the sea sparkled in silver and gold, like the ocean was covered in glitter."

The bar was glued to Big Daddy.

"The first body we saw was a woman who popped up right next to us. I was on the bridge and the guys were pretty reluctant to do anything about it. And then one of 'em, he fought in Viet Nam, had no problems handling the dead. He opened up the tuna door and pulled her right in. She was completely naked. It was pretty

17

bad, but we had to do what we had to do," said Big Daddy, his voice rasping off to a whisper.

"Go on," The Talker gleamed.

"The next thing we know there's a lot of shoes floating in the water. We pulled in a mail bag and a backpack with diapers in it. And then we pulled in a pair of shoes with feet in them. That was pretty rough."

Harvard winced.

"We got as close to the flames as we could, but it was the fumes that got to us, burned our eyes and made it hard to breath. For a while, we didn't find anything else and then suddenly, a couple of bodies popped up through the silver and gold like they just broke away from the wreckage. The one thing I'll never get out of my head was the look on their faces—sheer terror. One guy's hands were up like he was clenching the seat in front of him; had the most horrible look on his face. And everyone we pulled in, six altogether, were totally naked, clothes completely blown away."

The barflies listened with their mouths open.

Flight 800 had 230 passengers, including a French club headed for Paris from a high school in Pennsylvania. My mind envisioned their excitement when the trip was first announced and the anticipation leading up to their departure. Who could have ever imagined that of all the days and all the airlines and all the flights to France, this would be the one to crash into the ocean? I thought of the families left behind and the kids who wanted to go, but for whatever reason, could not.

"Pretty soon there were rescue boats everywhere pulling in what they could," Big Daddy started back up. "It was cat-and-mouse with the flames and more than once I had to throw her in reverse and back the hell out of there. There was a guy driving around with a body draped over his gunwales and that just wasn't right. I yelled at him to get it the hell off of there for Christ's sake."

"What'd you do with the bodies?" The Talker asked.

"We could have pulled in more, but the ones we had were starting to bleed out and it was a mess. We didn't want to start stacking 'em on top of each other, so we headed for shore. They told us to go to the Coast Guard Station and what a sight that was. Bodies were lined up on the docks like cordwood. Boats unloading and heading back out."

"God have mercy," muttered a voice.

"Once we pulled into the station, the authorities took over. They unloaded everything and decontaminated the boat. Then they decontaminated us, sprayed us with bleach, but the problem was they didn't have any water to rinse us off, so we stood there with the Clorox burning our privates. We decided not to head back out."

"It was a missile that brought her down wasn't it, Big Daddy?" The Talker kept him going. "TWA was blown from the sky."

"Terrorists, probably, or maybe it was the Navy doing some kind of exercise in the area and now it's one big cover up. All's I know is we saw something streak through the sky toward that plane and then we saw the explosion. It came down in burning pieces. Nobody had a chance."

CHAPTER 7

DESTINIES

I pictured myself on Flight 800. First the explosion and then the blast of frozen air as the plane broke apart. The screams and then falling, gasping. No wonder their faces were locked in horror. They all went quick, I hope, but I don't think it was instantaneous. They had split seconds of terror, aware of their violent death. Horrible, horrible thoughts in my head, numbed only by the drink.

"Who's up for another one," the barkeep broke in.

Everyone shoved in their glass.

My mind went to the time I was a newspaper reporter and a call came in about a collision between a car and a train. They sent me. My press pass got me by the yellow tape and I strode past the emergency workers, camera slung over my shoulder. It was one of the few unprotected railroad crossings left on Long Island, at the entrance to a junk yard. There were no automatic gates or flashing lights, only a series of large signs warning you to look both ways before you cross. On this day, the signs weren't enough. A hundred feet from the crossing was a smashed up sedan resting on the gravel and beyond it was a Long Island Rail Road diesel with a half dozen cars. I wanted to frame the car in a shot with the train in the background. Moving closer, I saw the driver sitting there, peacefully upright, with his hands still on the wheel. My head jerked back and turned to a policeman.

"He's quite dead," the officer said.

What transpired in this poor guy's life that put him at the crossing at that instant? A few seconds earlier, he would have crossed the tracks unscathed with nothing more than a scare. A few seconds later and he would have seen the train and stopped. But that was not his fate. Maybe he left the house earlier than planned. Maybe his wife was nagging him and he skedaddled out the back door without his glasses and couldn't see the signs. Was it his fault? Or maybe it was his time as God so determined it just like everything else, just like he did for John John and those poor souls on Flight 800.

The next accident I covered literally came to our front door. I was at the typewriter banging out the week's news when we were interrupted by screeching brakes and a sonic boom. Right in front of the building was a large work truck smashed up against a van. Gawkers appeared and among them, walking around in a daze, was none other than my mother's brother, my Uncle John.

"What the hell happened?"

"I was driving along and this guy comes into my lane and we hit head on," Uncle John said, his whole body shaking. The driver of the van was still inside, trapped. My uncle operated the Singing Tree service and was hauling a few tons of logs and wood chips in the back of his truck.

Cops blocked off the scene and then we noticed the skid marks. My uncle's truck had double wheels in the rear which left two sets of black marks veering away from the center line. There were no skid marks coming toward his. What made the incident so remarkable was about halfway through the skid, Uncle John's marks jumped over a foot to the right and kept going. This was the moment of impact. The truck hit the van head on, stopped it cold, and sent it back the other way, and in the process, it bounced one foot over and kept going. It took heavy rescue more than an hour to extricate the driver.

The next day I called the hospital to inquire about his condition. The operator put me on hold and then someone answered.

"Hello."

"Hello. This is Bob Chartuk with Suffolk Life Newspaper. I'm looking for the guy who was in the accident yesterday?"

"Yeah."

"Uuuh. How are you?"

"I'm pretty fucked up."

Incredibly, he was driving a van with a special wheelchair lift and no driver's seat. The guy had been paralyzed in an accident a few years earlier and was operating the van with hand controls while sitting in his wheelchair. He had fallen asleep at the wheel.

The few patrons left at the bar lost interest and I was about to head out when I noticed the Talker staring at me.

"You're a pretty interesting guy for such a douche," he said with the charisma that keeps people around him despite being as big a nobody as the rest of us. What I couldn't understand was why he was always out drinking and catting around when he had a pretty wife and three kids at home.

"Thanks, I think. What about you? You must have some interesting tales to tell."

"Nah, nothing I want to talk about." Lines crimped his boyish face as he dragged his cigarette.

"What about the time they hoisted Martin up on the flagpole? Weren't you in on that?"

"Yeah, that was pretty funny," The Talker coughed as he laughed. "The principal came out and lowered him down."

"It's funny, we all wish we could be back at school, do it all over again," I said.

"Not me, I'm good where I'm at."

"Come on, who wouldn't want another chance?"

"That school didn't give us a chance, just like this town didn't give us nothing," The Talker snapped.

"I don't know, I guess we can all make something of ourselves if we really wanted."

"You know what your problem is? You want to be too much like that fag, John Boy."

"You got that right," I answered. "Wouldn't you rather be rich and famous instead of sitting in this stinking bar?"

"Nah, I'm happy right here." He lit a cigarette off the one before.

I thought about the night during high school when we heard brakes screech up Bellevue Avenue. The driver couldn't stop and crossed over Main Street, hitting the guard rail on the other side. It was our neighbor's car and popping out unscathed was none other than The Talker, not even old enough to have a license. He was gone before the dust settled and the cops were soon on the scene. About 20 minutes later back came The Talker to admire his handiwork. We couldn't believe they didn't put two and two together and lock him up.

"Yeah, John dying screwed me up a little," I admitted. "We were the same age you know. He was born a month before me."

The Talker squinted. "You gotta let it go. Take what you got and live your life."

"And what life is that? Hanging out here all night with people like you?"

"There's the goddamn door. You can leave anytime you want, but I think you like it here, telling your stupid stories."

"Sad to say, my man, but those stories are all I got. Who are we anyway compared to a Kennedy? They have everything and we got nothing."

"You know why we ain't got nothing? It's because of this place, that's why. What's our town except a place to grow up and die? You have a dream and there's no hope for it. You end up like Jerry Duffy or those people falling from the fucking sky."

"Let me ask you, just wondering. You got a wife and kids. What are you doing here? Why don't you go home?"

"Why don't you kiss my ass?"

"Hey, I know I'm miserable, sitting here drinking my problems away. But what about you? You got a life. What's wrong with that?"

"Yeah, I got a life and you're a fucking asshole. Maybe that's want's wrong with that."

He threw back his stool and I braced for the attack.

"Just an asshole like everyone else around here."

He slammed down his glass and went out the door. I doubt he went home.

23

Chapter 8

ON THE WATER

Out at the Flight 800 crash site, Captain Wayne pulled us alongside the Rude and with the summer waves running about two feet it was a little tricky transferring the people and gear to the bigger ship. The captain said he would stay nearby and to radio when we were ready to go back. As he pulled away, his wake churned a strange swatch of silver and gold which grabbed our attention like an omen.

"We're right on top of the wreckage," Captain Sam DeBow told us up on the bridge. "It's spread out pretty wide, about 130 feet deep." The newsmen hung on his every word. "We use side-scan sonar to locate whatever's on the bottom," the Captain explained, his face glowing green from the light of the sonar screen. "We usually work in shipping lanes and harbors, but we can find anything that's down there. Look at this," he tapped his finger on the glass. "Most everything in nature is gradual and curvy. If you see a straight line and sharp corners, it's not supposed to be there."

A half dozen heads squeezed together to see a ghostly image with broken lines and corners pan across the screen. "That's a piece of the plane."

As I focused on the blurry images the feeling I was fighting since we first set foot on the boat got worse.

Goddamned seasick.

I backed out of the bridge as casually as I could and climbed down to the deck. In my own boat, I could crash over waves with no ill effects and have a good laugh at my passengers as I launched us through the air—as long as the boat kept moving. But a large platform, seemingly steady under your feet, harbors a devious secret: it's moving up and down ever so slightly. You can hardly tell you're in motion but your middle ear makes no sense of it at all. It's a feeling that makes death seem a reasonable alternative and I hated myself for not getting the pills. I've been on big boats before, a few times as the victim suffering in seasick hell, and others with a Dramamine buzz entertaining myself from the misery of those who wouldn't take it. It's usually the men who get the sickest, the ones who brag they don't need the little pill. I knew I needed it and was not ashamed to down as many as necessary. Unfortunately, I went for the black raspberry shake instead.

The ABC newsman filed his story from the bridge:

"This is Dan Johnson reporting from the Rude, a NOAA vessel here at the scene of the TWA Flight 800 crash. This is a special ship from the National Oceanic and Atmospheric Administration which usually patrols our harbors and ports to produce nautical charts. On this mission, out here about nine miles off of Moriches Inlet, it's using its capabilities to find the remains of the ill-fated flight."

The NOAA brass must have been proud.

"The Rude and its crew, who are part of our nation's uniformed services like the Army and the Navy, use a side-scan sonar called a fish to patrol the bottom."

The camera panned the deck to show the crew deploying the torpedo-shaped device.

"If anything's down there, they will find it and so far, they've found plenty, a debris field stretching more than a mile and maybe even longer before the night is through. It's a grim, but necessary task and the ship is playing a critical role in this, a massive recovery effort and now, a criminal investigation to find out what really brought down this 747. Reporting from the helm of the Rude at the crash site of TWA Flight 800, I'm Dan Johnson."

A public relations coup! Of all the assets at the crash site—Coast Guard, Navy, FBI, police—it was NOAA that gets the coverage, and right from its own ship in the middle of the action.

My bosses were so happy, they wanted me to do it all over again the following day.

Telling my story at the bar, I held attention of Big Daddy and the rest of them, but not of The Talker, who only dipped his head into the conversation at the end to hear my finale: When the camera panned the deck, you could see me in the background leaning over the rail. My tortured stomach couldn't hold the last thing to fill it, the black raspberry shake, which blasted out of me in a dark purple stream.

CHAPTER 9

PT-109

"With all this Kennedy talk going on, I decided to do some reading," Big Daddy piped up one smoky afternoon.

"Reading what?"

"The story about President Kennedy and PT-109."

"Let's hear it," the bar said in unison.

"They called them Patrol Torpedo boats and Kennedy skippered one of 'em during World War II. It was fitted out right in Brooklyn where the shipyards used to be. Thing was made of wood with three 12-cylinder Packards. Must have hauled ass, if you ask me. And it sported machine guns and depth charges and torpedoes. They even got rid of the life raft and replaced it with an antitank gun on the foredeck, according to what I was reading. Those were some serious mother fuckers."

Everyone sipped, eyes riveted to Big Daddy.

"Kennedy was going after the Japs in the Pacific near some little islands off New Guinea, but they got to him first. His PT was rammed by a Japanese destroyer and was cut in half. The boat exploded and the damn Japs kept right on going. Two men got killed instantly and the rest of 'em made it to a little island after about four hours. Goddamn lucky the sharks didn't get them first. They piled up on a big piece of wood that was left after the boat sunk and the men kicked it over to the island. Turns out, it was the freakin' wood they used to mount the antitank gun where the lifeboat was supposed to be. One of the wounded guys was floating on a lifejacket and Kennedy towed it by a rope in his teeth."

"How'd they make it?"

"The other PT boats saw it explode and didn't even go back for them thinking nobody made it. But they did and ended up on the little island which was so small there was nothing; no water, no coconuts, no nothing. So Kennedy swam a couple of miles to check out more islands and then brought his crew to one he found that had water, all the while laying low from the Japs."

Big Daddy guzzled his drink and went on:

"There was a big volcano on one of the islands and on top of it was an Australian, a coast watcher. He must have been shitting bricks the whole time because 10,000 Japs were stationed on the island right below him. He saw the explosion when the boat got rammed and sent two aborigines in a dugout canoe to go looking for survivors. They found them alright and Kennedy gave 'em a message he carved on a coconut shell which they brought to the PT base. Those two dudes paddled more than 40 miles to deliver that coconut. If the Japs caught 'em they would have killed 'em, probably tortured 'em first. The Navy came and rescued Kennedy and his crew six days later and it was a good thing too because they were in bad shape. Kennedy fucked up his back pretty good and could have gone home, but he didn't, no way. They put him in charge of another boat and he saved a group of Marines who got ambushed. One of them even died in Kennedy's bunk."

"Amazing."

"And you know what? Kennedy kept that little coconut on his desk when he was president."

There was more:

"JFK promised those two natives he would see them again and when he became president he invited them to the White House. They made the trip and when they got off the plane they were given the news. The president was shot dead. They turned around and went home and then you know what one of 'em did? Named his son John F. Kennedy in the president's honor, that's what. Years later, the Kennedy's came and bought 'em each a new house and a motor boat. When that little old man met the president's nephew he cried his eyes out. He's a freaking hero as far as I'm concerned."

Everybody sat quiet, contemplating their drinks.

"Try and top that," The Talker said over to me.

"I don't think I can top it, but I do have a story from my Dad from World War Two."

"Let's hear it."

My Dad followed in his older brother's footsteps and joined the Coast Guard in 1939. His first duty was patrolling New York Harbor and he said he was popular with the crew because he was the only one who knew how to cook. He was sent to radio school in Chicago and when the war broke out he was dispatched to the Dominican Republic to set up a secret radio station for the Navy. His brother was sent to the Pacific and fought the Japs hand-to-hand in the water at Guadalcanal.

The Navy was impressed by Coast Guard radiomen during prohibition when they monitored messages between the rumrunners and for the war, the operators were recruited for Naval intelligence. My Dad had expertise in electronics and boasted a solid 26 words-per-minute Morse code rating. He was well suited to spy on the Germans.

"We recorded all suspicious transmissions," he told me. "Spanish ships with their raspy spark transmitters and a South African station using the odd call sign *UU2*, which in Morse code sounded like the William Tell Overture. There was even a station operating out of Manhattan using the call sign *AOR* after the movie house on 92nd Street." He said the spies gave his dial a workout as they shifted frequencies throughout their messages.

"German Morse code was very precise and when you heard it, you knew it," he told me. "The hair would stand up on the back of your neck."

The Germans settled into a routine and Dad would wait for them to send their messages back to Hamburg. "I even took my breathing spells when they did," he said.

I asked him why the spy stations weren't hunted down and put out of business.

"What for? We intercepted and decoded all their messages, their harm neutralized," he explained. "Let's just say the Devil you know is better than the Devil you don't."

But there was one station he could never pin down. Its signal was faint and rarely came on. It went by the call letters *CEL*.

"His keying was slow," Dad said, "a couple of seconds between characters, making it easy to tune right past him when working the dial."

He set up a Dictaphone that operated on a wax cylinder and when they were testing it, a weak signal came through. The human ear could pick up little of it, but the recorder made out the dots and dashes. *CEL!*

Dad recoded the message, adding in some nonsense words to throw off the Germans, and relayed it to Washington.

Months went by until a special attaché landed on the island and presented him with a Navy Commendation medal, though they would not tell him what it was for. After the war he found out. *CEL* instructed a German submarine wolf pack to intercept a ship that was transporting U.S. soldiers across the Atlantic. It was the Queen Mary, sailing out of New Orleans, and aboard was an entire division, 1,500 men, heading for the battle in Europe.

The "Gray Ghost" was diverted and the lives were saved.

CEL was operating from a raft in the ocean and was silenced by a Navy destroyer.

"Good one," said Big Daddy. Even The Talker seemed impressed.

Years later, my Dad ran into a fellow veteran at a Memorial Day service and told him the story. The fellow's eyes welled up and he clutched my dad's hands, thanking him. "I was on that ship." he said.

Chapter 10

THE BUBBLE

A faint smell of burning oil accompanied us in the cockpit as we forced the Cessna through an unrelenting wind. Sitting next to me was Ken Eaton, a hanger mate of my buddies from the Sky Sailor's Glider School. I mentioned to the tow pilot that I had to make a trip to northern New York for my job with the weather service and he suggested, "Why not go with Ken? He'll let you fly and you can rack up some hours."

Sounded like a good idea.

When I arrived at Rust Avenue, Ken was outside checking his plane, a two-seat, single-engine Cessna which, like everything else at the hanger, looked as if its glory days were long passed.

"At least the belts are tight," he said, pulling his hand from the engine compartment. "Let's go."

He put on his radio headset and I instinctively did the same.

"Taxi out this way," he commanded, nodding toward a faded set of lines on the tarmac. "I'll handle the engine and when we get going, take it right up."

It dawned on me as I took hold of the yoke: *He thinks I know how to fly!* I took three glider lessons with Gruff, but had never even been in a small plane, much less flown one. But I was going with the flow, two trembling hands on the yoke and my feet shaking on the pedals.

"Go left and you'll be clear," he said as I moved the pedals to steer.

Take it right up, I thought to myself.

"Cessna 72738 clear to take off runway one nineteen," the tower crackled, prompting Ken to reach down to a little knob on the dash. He pulled it and the engine roared.

"Pull up at 65," said the pilot, tapping a gauge on the dashboard. *Does he have any idea I don't know how to fly?*

The plane bumped along and the needle marched to 65. I pulled up and off we went, my hands holding a death grip on the controls.

I was flying north to find a place to situate a new weather radar station in upstate New York. The locals were against it and my job was to win them over for a new technology that would give them better weather reports, albeit from a huge white dome towering 150 feet into the sky.

I stole a glance at Ken, whose nose was buried in a map.

"With this headwind, it's going to take us a while," the pilot said. "Might even have to stop for gas."

He referenced another gauge. "Altimeter's bouncing around, so try to keep it at thirty-five hundred."

The wind shoved the plane up and down like a toy kite and I fought the yoke to keep the needle at 3,500 feet.

Ken patted a small box at our knees. It was a transponder pinging our signal to the world.

"Air traffic's following our every move. Keeps us out of trouble. Wouldn't fly without it," he told me.

Our eyes flashed back to the altimeter, which had dropped to 3,000.

"Come on," Ken said. "Keep it steady. You don't want them to think you're an amateur. And keep it level," he added, pointing to a gauge with a pair of wings in it. The wings were tilted which meant I wasn't level.

"Keep your eyes on the altimeter and the wings and if you don't trust them, use the bubble."

Screwed to the dash was a device similar to the glass vial in a carpenter's level with a bubble of air in it. If the bubble was in the middle, you were level. If not, you were tilted to the opposite side.

"Okay, I'll watch the bubble."

Cessna 72738 droned through the sky over central New York and my hands were starting to cramp from gripping the yoke.

"Hold your altitude, three five zero zero, Cessna 72738," the air traffic controller cut into our headphones. Ken glared at me. The wind was pushing the plane up and down and I had all I could do to keep it steady. If I focused on the altimeter, I lost sight of the bubble and the plane would tilt. We were crabbing through the sky almost sideways to stay abreast of the wind and my foot hurt from jamming the pedal. Our progress was painfully slow.

"Looks like we're going to have to get some fuel," Ken said as he rustled the map. "Sky Park. We'll hit Sky Park. Compass 315."

I looked at the compass and we were heading due north, 360, so I nosed us a little to the left and pegged it at 315. Ken looked pleased.

Up ahead, the beautiful blue sky became a frightful black. We were flying into a snow squall.

"Better let me take it," Ken said, as I felt him grab the other yoke. The tranquil countryside vanished as white streaks struck the windshield. The bubble danced in its little tube.

"Pull up, pull up Cessna 72738," demanded the voice in our ears. "Go around."

Ken yoked the steering column toward him and gunned the engine. Despite the whiteout, I could see the dark terrain rushing beneath us.

Ken said nothing as he climbed and looped back, his face red and sweaty.

"Steady in," the controller said.

"Okay, okay."

The runway shot up at us and I braced for impact. Ken stamped on the pedals like he was putting out a fire and the yoke bounced in his hands. At the last second, he got the wings level and touched us down true and straight.

There's a feeling you get when you know it's not your time. Out of gas, blinded by snow, I thought our chances of ending up dead were pretty good. Yet I knew we were going to make it. I can't explain why. I just knew.

Fueled up, and with the squall blown through, we headed back out under sunny skies. Our final destination was the Watertown International Airport, but don't let the lofty designation fool you, it was no JFK. I was to join a team from Washington to meet with officials of Montague, N.Y., a town on the leeward side of Lake Ontario which gets hit with some of the greatest snowfall in America. The team watched us taxi in and then we were off in a rental car driving in channels plowed through huge drifts of snow. Before we even left the airport, the driver slid off the road and wedged us into a snow bank. We all got out to push. A minute later, he did it again.

"I'm from California," he admitted. "What do I know about driving in snow?"

We switched drivers and were soon traversing the desolate countryside to a place called the Tug Hill Plateau. The white drifts I saw from the air were now at eye level and surrounded us all the way to the address of the Supervisor of the Town of Montague. His home was his farm and we were welcomed into a house that was attached to a huge barn. He was a dairy farmer who supplied his product to Kraft for Philadelphia brand cream cheese.

Introductions around and we explained the reason for our visit: The weather radar at Fort Drum had to be moved and the Town of Montague, east of the great lake, would be a perfect location for the government to maintain a uninterrupted chain of Doppler radars to protect northeast America.

"What's in it for us?" he asked.

"Better weather forecasts."

"What do we care? If it snows it snows."

While we talked, we were distracted by the sound of chirping birds and I thought it rather odd, the sound being so loud inside the Supervisor's living room.

"I'll see what I can do," he said of our request to have the town's planning and zoning departments sign off on the project. We were the federal government and didn't need local approval, but it was Washington's policy not to ruffle the feathers of our host communities.

As we were leaving, I peered into the kitchen to see what was making all the noise. In the middle of the floor was a plastic kiddie pool filled with hundreds of little, yellow chickens.

Back at Watertown, my colleagues queued up for their commercial flight and, I have to say, I felt pretty special walking out through a restricted area to the plane I was going to fly back home. I brought her up into a glorious sunset with a breeze at our back. It was a delight not fighting the wind home and I had no problem keeping the bubble in the middle and the altitude steady. In fact, we heard little from air traffic control as the lights of little towns flickered past. My hand resting comfortably on the yoke and no pressure on the pedals, I permitted my mind to wander.

With the Montague radar, we could complete our chain of weather towers in the northeast. People would be safer. They would be warned of thunderstorms and tornados by state-of-the-art radars, a vast improvement over the previous equipment which, to the nation's embarrassment, used antiquated vacuum tubes that were only available from the Soviet Union. Imagine, weather reports for our country relying on parts from Russia.

I thought back to the huge tornado that struck Alabama. I was sent as part of a disaster survey team and arrived the day after it hit. We were cleared by the police into an area where it looked like a bomb exploded. Trees stripped of leaves and bark scored the sky. Pieces of homes dangled from broken limbs and everything was speckled in black grit. Crisscrossing the devastation were perfectly straight dirt roads and I asked the sheriff why they didn't pave the streets in these parts. He said they did, just that the tornado sucked up all the asphalt and obliterated it.

I saw a man wandering in a daze.

"I'm Bob Chartuk with the National Weather Service," I introduced myself. "Do you mind if I ask you about the storm?"

"I'll tell ya," he said. "They all laughed when I built my tornado shelter. They ain't laughing now."

Thirty six people were killed.

Another man told me of the couple next door who the neighbors disliked because when everyone was home watching TV, they were blasting their stereo. When the storm came every station carried the warning and people took cover. Everyone except this couple, and just before the tornado hit, they put their three-year-old daughter in the dryer. The sheriff found her crying 250 yards away, still inside the machine. Her mom and dad were killed.

I felt proud to be part of an agency that made people safer, but there was always a nagging problem: Bad weather happens, and no matter how much you warn them, people are still going to die in tornadoes, blizzards, floods, and thunderstorms. And whose fault is that?

Up ahead, I could see the lights of the coast ending and the black expanse of the Long Island Sound stretching across the horizon. Lights of ships were visible below. My mind was gripped by the ASOS problem.

The Automated Surface Observing System was a controversial part of the weather service modernization. Prior to the rise of ASOS, human beings across the country, particularly at airports, would go outside every hour and report what they saw. Even with weather satellites, Doppler radar stations, advanced computer and communications systems—all the tools of our modernized weather world—nothing beats a human observer, especially when it comes to visibility, a chief concern of pilots.

The weather service was roundly criticized for the ASOS setup, especially the visibility problem and its use of an automated voice to report the conditions. Where you once had a human reporting the weather, you now had a machine. I must admit, it was nice listening to the weather radio at night and hear the sweet voice of a girl I knew giving me the weather. News articles had me defending the ASOS, which was described as sounding like a drunken Arnold Schwarzenegger. While pilots argued the ASOS didn't do a very good job reporting fog and haze, they all knew the truth: It cost a lot to pay people to report the weather and sooner or later, the human would succumb to the machine.

The water of the sound was black slate compared to the sparkling lights of Long Island and approaching Gabreski Airport, I wondered why the runways were so dark.

"Watch this," said Ken as he adjusted the radio. "We can turn the lights on from here." Like Dorothy in the Wizard of Oz, he clicked the mic three times and the airport lit up like a Christmas tree.

"Wow."

I guided us down toward the middle of the lights and Ken smiled admirably. The trick is to let the plane glide in and touch down as it lowers ever so slightly from the sky. Unfortunately, I didn't fully grasp the concept and felt I could expedite the process by pushing the yoke forward. Rather than land like a feather, the maneuver bounced us off the runway and jerked the plane sideways with an alarming chirp of the tires. Maybe it was the hours I spent jamming the foot pedals to keep our plane crabbing north, or maybe it was the stick and pedal of my glider flights, but as the plane jolted right, I instinctively corrected with pedal left. Miraculously, the plane straightened, and I got us down. I ventured a sheepish look at Ken. He looked like he didn't know if he should hug me or kill me.

CHAPTER 11

SANDY

"I think he was a faggot," The Talker proclaimed one night.

"Who?" as if I didn't know.

"John John."

"You're out of your freaking mind."

The Talker really knew how to piss me off and if I had to give him credit for something, he was persistent.

"That's right. Did you ever see the pictures of him peddling his bike around in those tight shorts? Now who the hell wears tight little shorts unless you're gay or something?"

"Guys who ride bikes wear them, you idiot."

"Screw you, fuck head. All's I know is when I ride a bike I don't wear faggy-looking shorts."

"Why don't you give the guy a break?

"Why don't you kiss my ass?"

"Now, now, you two," a voice rose between us. It was soft and sweet and came from a goddess who floated into the Sports Page bar to rescue me. She was tall and blond and willowy and beautiful.

"I'm Sandy," her blue eyes penetrated. "I've been hearing about your stories."

The Talker intervened. "I'm Danny. I haven't seen you here before."

"I usually don't go to bars, but a friend of mine said there was some interesting conversation going on and I guess she was right."

"A drink for the lady," Danny commanded as he wedged between us.

"So, you have trouble telling queers apart from straight people," she teased Danny. The bar snickered as Sandy craned her head around him. "You're Bob, right? Dee said you're always here telling some crazy stories."

"Oh, yes, Dee. She's your friend?" I swallowed hard. Danny squinted at me with a look of death and swooped in again.

"Bobby Boy's all bent out of shape over Kennedy and has some kind of weird attraction to the guy."

"You're the jealous one," I countered. "You keep bringing him up."

"That's because you're so…"

"Alright already," Sandy cut in. "I didn't come here to listen to this. Let's get a table," she said, grabbing my arm. I threw Danny a sneer as we walked away. He shook his fist at me.

"I met him once," Sandy offered as we settled in. "I was walking toward the Museum of Modern Art and he was on his bike. You wouldn't have known it was him. He had a helmet on, sunglasses, and yeah, pretty tight shorts. He was peddling like he was racing the world. But he had to stop for traffic and the photographers were right behind him on bicycles, motorcycles, cars, clicking away. He took it all in stride, casually sipping from his water bottle, like he was posing for a magazine."

"Pretty weird. The guy picks his nose and it's on the front page of every paper."

"I know. So there I was, waiting to cross, and he says, 'Hi ya doing?' and I say, 'pretty good,' and the light turns green and off he goes. Did you ever meet him?"

"It's a long story."

"I have all night."

CHAPTER 12

THE NATIONAL ENQUIRER

For as long I can remember, my mother read the tabloids and growing up, they were always in the house. We read the National Enquirer and the Star and the Weekly World News until it got too weird. Every week, they piped the world of the glitterati into our mundane lives—celebrity gossip with paparazzi shots of famous people and lurid stories of their personal lives. Like gawkers at an accident, we couldn't get enough. Stuck in Center Moriches, secluded from the real world, I could live my life vicariously, in weekly increments, through John F. Kennedy, Jr.

"Do you think he got drunk? I mean, do you think he would go in a bar and tie one on," I blathered.

"I guess so. I don't think he sat home."

"You think his friends gave him a hard time?" I babbled. "Here's the sexiest man alive and he goes out drinking with his buddies. Do you think anyone's going to break his chops?"

"Probably not," Sandy twirled her straw. "What do you think about the Madonna thing?"

"I don't know, do you mean, what?"

"You know, she wanted to be as famous as Marilyn Monroe and her coup de grace was snagging the young John John just like Marilyn did the father."

"Wow, that's heavy." I felt my face flush. It hit me that my interest in the guy was pathetic, just like the rest of the gawkers. I fed off John Kennedy like a hysterical fan, not once seeing how the madness affected him.

"I couldn't imagine growing up like that," I said, my mind now sympathizing with his hounded soul. Could Sandy read the guilt in my face? By absorbing him every week, I helped fuel the industry that tortured him.

"Well, it didn't seem to faze him," Sandy went on. "At least he had the courage to live his life, celebrity be damned."

Would I have wilted under the scrutiny? I wondered to myself.

"Remember when they got into that fight in Central Park?" Sandy asked.

"Yeah, there was a video of it. Carolyn and John having a fight for all the world to see."

"It was an international sensation. Two lovers having an argument, but because it's them, the whole world tuned in."

"I have a story of crazy love. Want to hear it?"

"Pray tell," said the goddess of the Sports Page Bar and Restaurant.

One night my girlfriend got drunk and didn't want me to leave her by herself. We were together all that day and the day before and, I'm sure, all waking hours back to the day we met. I wanted her to go to bed and sleep it off so I could go home by myself. She would have none of it, as if I would be gone forever if I walked out the door. First her assaults were verbal, terrible, drunken things—I was shocked how my angel could turn so wicked.

"Get the hell out and don't ever come back," she screamed with such venom.

But when I went to leave, she felt the need to punish me instead.

I made a dash for the door and she jumped on my back, twirling us around like sitcom characters. We bounced off a wall and fell to the floor, her fists drumming my head. I turned us around and pinned her. "What's wrong with you?" I yelled. She spit in my face.

Thankfully, there was no video.

I broke free and ran out the door, my soul mate in hot pursuit. *Keys!*

A quick pat of my pockets forced me to Plan B: Keep running. The two of us bolted down the street, her anger nipping at my heels. Sheer terror kept me going and after a hundred-yard dash, she fell back and gave up, but not after spewing a stream of profanity that would've impressed a mobster. Horrified, I saw the lights of the neighbors blink on.

I skulked around the bushes into the wee hours until finally, driven by exhaustion and thirst, returned to her house through the neighboring back yards.

The scene was heartbreaking. The antenna and mirrors were snapped off my car and from the trunk, all of the Christmas presents I bought for her were torn open and strewn, wrapping paper and all, across the road. Everything was broken and stomped in a holy rage.

"Did you have the courage to leave her?"

"No," my head dropped toward my drink. "I couldn't do it. We stayed together and guess what? It happened again."

"What!"

"This time it was at my place after I meekly suggested she should go home for the night. The hate came out so violently she threw the TV at me."

"A portable?"

"No. It was pretty big set. I don't know how she even lifted it. But she got her arms around it and heaved it at me. It exploded all over the floor."

"Damn, you must have done something to really piss her off."

"No, I just wanted to be alone for a while."

"I felt that way about someone once," Sandy said gazing up at the ceiling. "I loved him so much I couldn't bear the thought of him leaving, even if it was just for a night."

"Did you make love to him?" It was the boldest question I ever asked.

"Yes. Yes and I think that was it. He fulfilled me so completely I couldn't have wanted anything else."

"You gave him the most precious thing you had."

"Yes, and he should have been damned glad and paid for it the rest of his life," she said, slamming down her glass.

"You made love to her?" Sandy asked back.

"Yes, just the way you said."

"Incredible, right?"

"At first she wouldn't, like she knew how it would end. She cried after we did it and I was pretty confused. Why would she be mad after we felt so good?"

"She was afraid, afraid it wouldn't last."

"So when I wanted to go home…"

"It was like losing you forever. She gave you her soul and you would walk away from it?"

"Well, that explains the violence," my thoughts dredged back to the broken presents.

"So you finally found the courage?"

"My mind was made up from the first time she tried to kill me, but I dragged it out for a few more weeks. I finally told her over the phone when I was in another state. Found out she dated pretty much every friend we had after that."

Right then, in the dim lights of the tavern, it hit me: Sandy looked like Daryl Hannah, one of John's most celebrated crushes. Their relationship was perfect: Hollywood meets Camelot, and now Daryl's twin is sitting with me. My face felt hot.

"What do you think about Daryl Hannah?" I asked.

"I know she was hot and heavy with John."

"You look just like her," I gushed.

"No way. You really think so?"

"You could be her twin. Tall, blond, beautiful."

"You're such a flirt."

CHAPTER 13

THE MAGNETS

My time with Sandy in the boozy confines of the Sports Page was exactly what I needed to carry me through my funk. She was interested in me and my stories and even invited some of her friends to join us. To Danny's chagrin, evenings would find me holding court in the back room and the bartender didn't mind as long as the drinks kept flowing. I entertained the crowd and relished the stardom. They mostly wanted to hear about John John, though I squeezed in some stories of my own. After losing John, I thought more and more about death and how we will all meet our fate someday. I fretted over why, in the blink of an eye, some of us will perish so tragically, and why others, so undeserving, go on.

"You seem hung up on death and gory accidents," Sandy said one night.

"There's a reason and if you don't want to be my psychiatrist, I understand."

"Don't mind at all. Let it all out if you have to."

It started when I was a little boy, maybe six or seven. My family home is situated on Main Street, at a sharp curve in the road at the border of East Moriches and Center Moriches. Eons ago, an Indian probably followed an old animal path which, for reasons known only to Mother Nature, made a quick jog to the south before straightening and eventually going all the way to the end of Long Island. This caused no problems for a millennia, until the advent of the automobile. The elbow is preceded on both sides by straight-aways which have traffic rushing, unexpectedly, into a "Deadman's Curve."

My first memory of the accidents came late one night when I was awakened by my brother's voice. He had dialed the operator for help. Across the street, I saw a chunk of metal accordioned against a tree. These were the days when vans had only a flat windshield between the occupants and the road ahead. The van was carrying a load of wood which had flung forward, crushing the driver against a maple tree. I gasped when I saw him and it was the last thing he ever heard. He reached a bloody hand to me and whispered, "Help me," before dropping limp. Backing away I heard my brother yell, "look," and we saw a dark figure in the middle of the road. It was a passenger who had been thrown clear and was laying, quite dead, on the black pavement.

"Oh man, that's gory," said a voice from a group that was listening in. "Enough of that!"

"No. Tell us more," said another.

The worst crash happened about two years after the van. This time, the impact threw me out of bed and I ran outside to see what happened. A convertible found the tree next to the one hit by the van and the occupants were twisted into the metal. Wailing sirens came and the scene was bathed in the red glow of emergency flares. There, on the street, something struck me about car crashes: With their smoky mix of gas, hot oil, and antifreeze, they all smell the same.

The crew mopped up the tragedy as the wee hours ticked away and most traces, except for some glittering glass and stains, were swept aside. I went back to bed, but as soon as the night's horror drifted from me, I was startled awake again by a new wave of sirens and lights—same cops, same firemen, same location. Turns out, there weren't two souls in that car, but three. They found him, dead, in the field about 100 feet away.

Screeching tires in my neighborhood would have us brace for impact, or we would resolve the tension with, "He made it." Sometimes the ferocity of the crash would have us dial for help before even looking to see what happened. The bad dreams of my youth featured vehicles cart-wheeling toward me, slapping me awake at the moment of impact. The crashes were such a part of our neighborhood that one night some of my sister's friends decided to fake one. They put their car against one of the scarred trees and laid out on the hood and it was good and funny until a cop happened by and chased them away.

One day, the carnage came right at me. I had teamed up with our mentally impaired neighbor, Allan, who we called Elvis, because in one of his larks, he dressed up like The King of Rock and Roll and paraded up and down Main Street with fake sideburns and a beat up guitar. He didn't know how to play it, but tried real hard. Once, a friend of my sister's, I think one of the guys from the fake crash, put a firecracker between the strings and lit it. Elvis started strumming like mad yelling, "I'm making sparks!"

Bang, the firecracker went off and scared the hell out of him. Broken strings dangling from the guitar, Elvis chased after us swinging it wildly. We laughed so hard we could hardly outrun the big oaf.

Me and Elvis hatched a plan to steal some of my dad's Schaefer beer and sell it from a card table instead of Kool-Aid like normal kids. Every time a car went by, we held up a sign: "Beer." We had some customers too, and I handled the money, which was fine with Elvis because he helped himself to the beer. I was 11 and Elvis was a teenager who had gotten his first taste of the suds. He had recently transitioned from his Elvis phase and was now the Fuhrer in a beat up army coat throwing "Heil Hitlers" at the neighborhood kids. Elvis was a big lummox compared to the younger boys and would hang around talking nonsense and smoking cigarettes when we had our backyard football games. Once, we coaxed him into playing, but the joke was on him: We tipped off the other side that it was Elvis up the middle and when he got the ball everybody jumped on him yelling, "Dog pile on the rabbit," like in the Bug's Bunny cartoon. When we all peeled off, he laid there gasping for breath with his face in the dirt. We thought we killed him.

So Elvis is getting drunk and Heil Hitlering passing cars and I'm raking in pocket change selling my dad's beer when our attention is gripped by an out of control pickup truck coming around Deadman's Curve. It bumped into the car in front of it and swerved onto the sidewalk a mere two feet from our stand. Rushing past, the truck blasted sand into our eyes and blew our hair back. It mowed down the neighbor's hedge, bounded across his lawn, and crashed into Jack the Eel Man's car which dominoed into his house. The impact roused the neighborhood which converged on the scene like a mob with pitchforks. We sat frozen in our folding chairs with our mouths open and I'm not sure if Elvis dribbled beer on his lap or peed his pants. The driver, a grizzled old black man with white hair, spilled out of the truck still clutching his bottle.

"The toilet paper got caught under the brake," he appealed to the crowd, his bloodshot eyes wild. "It was the toilet paper."

"Toilet paper my ass," the Eel Man replied. "You're drunk."

Another drunk was Elvis, who felt compelled to drape his arm around me as we walked back to our booth. His breath smelled like an empty beer can with a cigarette in it.

"I thought we we're going to die, man," he stammered as he leaned more of his bulk onto me. "Goddamn, I thought we were dead. That fucking guy would have killed us." I couldn't break free from his trembling girth. "Fuck, fucking goddamn it. We were dead."

We shuffled a few more steps. "Shit, fucking shit!" the pseudo dictator cried out as he collapsed. It took all my young strength to steer us off the sidewalk and plant Elvis onto the bushes that were flattened by the truck. He started to puke and I ran into the house. I hid in my room until my mother hounded: "Get that stuff off the sidewalk before your father gets home." I peeked out the window to see if it was safe. Elvis was still lying in the bushes.

Not wanting to catch hell for taking the beer, I headed out the backdoor and up the driveway to close up shop. Just as I got to the sidewalk, I again heard the screeching of tires. From the same direction as the drunken Negro, another maniac fish-tailed at me. At the last second, as if pulled by a magnet, the car careened away and crashed into one of the familiar trees across the street. Jarred out of his stupor by the impact, Elvis crawled into our back yard and I ran into the house and stayed put, not even joining the onlookers. My mother, God bless her, put away the beer stand before Dad got home.

"That's crazy," said a voice from the audience. "What a place to live."

"Tell them about Ed Metski," another called out and my face froze.

My high school year book is dedicated to my friend Ed Metski, who died with a couple of our other schoolmates in a horrible crash. I would have been in that car, except for my Dad insisting I be in by nine on school nights. I had hell to pay a few times for coming home late and this night I was determined to make it on time. My friends stopped and asked if I wanted a ride. It was five minutes to and I was five minutes away and I didn't want to blow the curfew. I passed. They were headed to the rolling hills of Dayton Avenue, a popular stretch of road for joy riders, and wouldn't have dropped me off at my house, I'm sure. Speeding over one of the hills, they became airborne and crashed into a tree roof first. Ed and the others were crushed.

"Can you stand some more?" I looked out at my audience.

"You're on a roll."

One groggy morning before school, eleventh grade, I was sitting at the kitchen table when the screech of tires snapped my head from my cereal. I had a clear view of the curve of death and saw a car hit the guard rail and a blur fly through the air landing on the neighbor's lawn. I was the first on the scene. It was just me and the driver and the smoldering smell. His flight through mortality wasn't kind and he lay there with a large hole in his head. I could see his brain. I ran back into the house and grabbed the blanket off my bed. My morning visitor was motionless, so I covered his body with my blanket as the sirens pierced the morning air.

"No way."

"Sick."

But the story doesn't end there. Years later I was at the Triangle Pub in Eastport when I noticed a fellow with a familiar scar across his skull.

"I bet I know how you got that," I nodded toward him.

"What?"

"That scar. I know how you got it, in Center Moriches, right? The scar rose as his eyes widened. It was in the exact outline of the hole I remembered in his head.

"You were in a wreck right in front of my house in Center Moriches. I saw the whole thing."

"Holy crap, man. You're right. They had to put a metal plate in my head," he said, tapping his noggin.

"I saw your brain. I thought you were dead."

"Nope. I'm fine. You saw my brain? Goddamn."

"Yup. I took the blanket off my bed and put it over you. I thought you were a goner."

"Whoa. Let me buy you a drink. Bartender, anything he drinks, on me. This dude saved my life."

Later on, I was sitting quietly with Sandy, exhausted from dredging up all the accident stories, but I felt okay, still in one piece. She put her hand over mine and looked into me with her beautiful eyes: "What if Flight 800 had blown up over Center Moriches?"

CHAPTER 14

LOVES LOST

"Did she want you to marry her?" Sandy asked one night as the crowd thinned out.

"Who?" I pretended.

"The girl who kept beating you up."

"Absolutely, but I was afraid."

"Afraid to commit?"

"Afraid to commit and afraid to break up. I knew we wouldn't last."

"And so did she."

"I'm glad she finally let me go."

"What if Carolyn let John go?"

"I don't know. After the fight in the park I imagine he had second thoughts. He probably wanted to move on, but didn't."

"He didn't have the courage?"

"He had the courage. That's why he married her, right or wrong. I admire him for making the decision."

"So if he didn't marry Carolyn, he'd be alive today?"

"That's a tough one," I pondered. "Maybe he would have died sooner. Maybe he would have been hit by a train. Crippled, disfigured, murdered. Who knows?"

"Maybe she pushed him into flying that night and he didn't have the courage to fight back."

"It looks like he fought back in Central Park, that's for sure."

"Maybe he was afraid and she pushed him," Sandy persisted. "Maybe he wanted to drive, but it would have taken too long and she wanted to get there sooner. She wanted to fly, he didn't."

"Or maybe he pushed her to go. Whatever the case, I'm just thinking it was their time and this was going to happen no matter what."

"He put them in that plane and crashed it into the water," Sandy's eyes narrowed.

"He did and that chain of events, every decision he made, every one of them—marrying Carolyn, learning to fly, getting in the plane, maybe they were all set in motion by God and poor John, he had no choice."

"But he did have a choice."

"Yeah, and what if the president lived? What if Oswald missed? What if Air Force One crashed with the entire family on it? Jesus Christ, I just don't know."

I stared at her. She was all the women in John John's life molded into one.

"I just can't get over the Madonna thing," Sandy backtracked.

"How's that?"

"Did you ever see her Material Girl video? She prances around the stage exactly like Marilyn Monroe, right down to the dress and flipping around a fan."

"I never made the connection."

"Marilyn did the same number in the movie, *Gentlemen Prefer Blonds*, singing *Diamonds Are a Girl's Best Friend*. Madonna completely rips her off and then set her sights on John John. It's all about the publicity with her. She shows up at the Grammy's with Michael Jackson and now she's working on Camelot. She must think it's her freaking destiny."

"I wonder what Jackie O thought about it?"

"Jackie O!" Sandy burst out, catching the attention of the bar. "Jackie O must have been totally pissed off. Her John with that tramp! Image her thinking that she was going to steal her son like Marilyn stole her husband? She probably thought Marilyn had come back from the dead."

Sandy couldn't be stopped: "Did you ever see her book, *Sex?* I couldn't imagine John keeping up with that. Lesbians, interracial sex, S and M, multiple partners. He probably looked like a deer in the headlights with her."

"I'm not sure of that," I wedged in. "I bet he could hold his own."

"Yeah, right. It was like an exhibitionist with a school boy. Plus, she was married to Sean Penn at the time. Jackie probably wanted to kill her."

"They would have made a pretty interesting couple, you gotta admit."

"I'll tell you who would have made a good couple. John and Brooke Shields."

"Brooke Shields?"

"That's right. She had that perfect look for him—beautiful but innocent. Not a headline stealing trollop like Madonna."

"I liked Daryl Hannah the best, actually."

"You may have a point there," Sandra conceded. "That match had it all: the world's most eligible bachelor and the beautiful blond movie star. Camelot and Hollywood. After she dumped that creep Jackson Browne, Daryl and John were inseparable. They moved in together and he even visited her on the set of her movie, *Attack of the 50-Foot Woman*. She was at his side when Jackie O died."

I imaged being attacked by a 50-foot Daryl Hannah.

"John also went out with Appolonia, Prince's main squeeze," Sandy went on.

"How do you know all of this?"

"You're not the only one who reads the National Enquirer."

Sandy launched into a catalogue of John's exploits, starting with the actresses.

"Besides Daryl, John was linked with Melanie Griffith, Sarah Jessica Parker, Catherine Oxenberg, Julia Roberts, Sharon Stone, Molly Ringwald…"

"Hold it! You're making this stuff up just to piss me off."

"I'm not trying to piss you off."

"Children! Behave," The Talker cut in. "Trust me. She's not trying to piss you off."

"John got invited to Cindy Crawford's 21ˢᵗ birthday party and dated her after that," Sandy just couldn't help herself. "I guess she left such an impression that John had her dress up like George Washington for the cover of his new magazine."

I looked at her and shook my head.

"There was also Claudia Schiffer, Janice Dickinson, Ashley Richardson..."

"I'm out of here."

"Don't forget Elle MacPherson and Stephanie of Monaco," Sandy said giggling with The Talker.

"He even nailed Princess Diana," The Talker shouted to the slamming door.

CHAPTER 15

I'LL KILL YOU

I drifted off to sleep and Sandy's deep blue eyes appeared in my dreams.

"I'm never going to let you go," she whispered to me.

She saw the panic on my face.

"Oh, take it easy, Baby Boy, I don't mean it that way. You're just an interesting guy and I like your company. Plus, I'm..."

She didn't finish the sentence.

We went to the back lot of the Sports Page which was unlit and dark. Sandy was parked all the way at the end under some trees. Her car smelled of perfume and I was intoxicated by the moment. Our lips came together and a flood of passion spilled out from both of us. I wanted to go slow and drink her in as long as the night would let me. My hands cupped her face as I kissed her and I ran my fingers across her neck. She shuddered. I pulled her tighter and kissed her harder, our tongues mashing out words not needed to be spoken.

Sandy's blond hair glowed by the dashboard light and I couldn't help to think how much she looked like Daryl. Her skin was white and immaculate and her legs were thin and long as they spread across my body. I ran my fingernails up and down her skin chasing waves of goose bumps across her sides to her front. Her breasts were large and taut and her nipples were hard as pebbles. She cried out when I squeezed them. Her lips nibbled their way across my neck generating chills that focused where my body met hers. She was wet and inviting and our throes of passion made me delirious, our bodies heaving together in perfect sync. Sandy's sighs coincided with her breathing and they quickly turned to gasps. She moaned harder with every breath and her sighs turned to cries and they kept coming louder and louder.

"Oh John," she breathed and then bang, a loud thump came from the hood of the car.

"Come out of there you son of a bitch. I'll kick your fucking ass," a distorted face screamed at the window.

Sandy leaped off.

"Your husband?" I whispered in panic.

"No, I think its Danny."

"You scum bag. I'll fuck you up," he hammered his fists on the roof.

Sandy threw the car into reverse and squealed out of the parking lot with the crazed fellow waving his arms after us.

"I'll kill you."

CHAPTER 16

ASOS

It was quite a while before I had any interest in returning to the Sports Page Bar and Restaurant. I crept through the back door and to my disgust, at our table in the back, sat Danny and Sandy.

"Hello stranger," Sandy smiled. Danny threw me his glare of death.

"Where have you been?" she chirped as if everything was fine.

Dandy seized the moment. "It was the ASOS, wasn't it?"

I looked at him in shock.

"Your ASOS system killed him," he hissed like he was throwing a dart.

"What?"

"I've been doing some research. Your little weather machines don't work and he wasn't warned about the fog. He flew into the fog and that's why he crashed."

John was flying under visual flight rules that night and because he wasn't quite ready for instrument flying, needed to see where he was going. But thanks to a thick summer haze draped over the water, he couldn't see a thing.

"Nobody told him about the fog and your ass-sauce gadget couldn't pick it up," he sneered. "So, when you add it all up, you killed him."

"Where the hell did you get that from?"

"The National Enquirer."

"The National Enquirer! Are you out of your freaking mind?"

"Nope. They had a big story about it. And it's pretty obvious. If he knew about the fog he never would have taken off. And if he never took off he wouldn't have crashed and you wouldn't be here talking up all your bullshit stories."

I looked at Sandy and she shook her head. I couldn't help but think she agreed.

I lunged after him, but our friends saw it coming and stopped me in my tracks. Danny was grabbed too.

"Let me go," I struggled against the hands. "I'll kick your fuckin' ass."

"I'll kick yours."

Harvard led me out the door and I stormed off into the night.

CHAPTER 17

THE SNOW RECORD

Sometimes you get lucky and God hands you a gift in the strangest of ways. But you have to be alert to hear the message. Our mission to relocate the weather service radar in upstate New York was not going well. The Montague locals weren't too enthusiastic and the opposition that reared up in other parts of the country followed us there. Making matters worse, the guy in charge of maintaining the radar at Fort Drum didn't want to travel the extra miles to a new location and was fanning the flames against us. Washington was getting antsy.

Then, from the sky, fell the Mother of all Snowstorms. Streaming off Lake Ontario and right into the Tug Hill Plateau came 77 inches—more than six feet of snow—in 24 hours, and a hell of a lot more after that. Montague was buried. It was a new record for the most snow in a single day. And the guy who measured it was a volunteer snow spotter for none other than our agency, the National Weather Service. In the world of people interested in this sort of thing—scientists, weather buffs, snowmobilers—he was an instant hero. I gave him a call.

"Your country needs you," I told him. "The people of Montague need the radar for accurate weather reports. You gotta know how much snow is coming your way and the radar will tell you. You can make this happen."

I asked him if he would make our case to the locals and he agreed. "I'll see what I can do." This coming from the guy who measured the most snowfall ever in a single day in America, I liked our chances.

Soon after, I got a call from Washington. The State of Colorado, home to the National Climatic Data Center and ground zero for some of the most rabid weather wizards on the planet, held the previous record for the most snow in one day and wasn't going down without a fight. They took exception to the measurements made by our Man in Montague. I pleaded our case. "Look, this guy's clearing the way for the radar—he's on our side. You can't pull the rug out from under him now."

The Washington bureaucrats resorted to the time-honored technique of not winning the argument with facts, but by attacking the opponent. And in this case, their biggest obstacle in saving the record for Colorado was me.

How dare I stuck my nose into something of such importance?

"I'm just trying to get the radar sited."

"You're clearly trying to jeopardize our standing with the entire meteorological community."

"Isn't the radar important for public safety?"

"Who are you to question us?"

I almost got fired over it.

A swat team of weather experts was dispatched to Montague.

"Oh brother," I said to the few friends I had left in Washington. "We're a week away from the town approving the radar and this guy's our ace in the hole. Are they going out of their way to blow this?"

I felt like a pea bouncing around the gears of government and I pictured a group of nerds in thick glasses slapping our Man in Montague with a snow-encrusted mitten.

"Take it back, you swine! You didn't really measure 77 inches, now did you?"

Just when my faith in humanity was at its lowest, two people rose up to restore it: Our snow spotter who, despite getting screwed out of his snow record, delivered for his country and got the radar approved, and a fellow I worked with in the radar program, John Porter, who told the D.C. brass to get off my back.

The swat team filed a report. It turns out Montague measured the snow six times over the 24-hour period, when he should have only measured it four times. Thus, the Tug Hill record is null and void and the U.S. title for the most snowfall in a day stays with Silver Lake, Colorado, which had 76 inches in 1921. I wonder how many freaking times they measured it back then. And of course, the committee recommended creating another committee to make sure these kind of climatic calamities never happen again.

CHAPTER 18

MONTEL

Of the 123 radar towers we were building, most were welcomed by their host communities, which appreciated the need for better weather information, not to mention the prestige of having a multi-million dollar federal facility in their midst. But in the areas that were against us, we were confronted by some real doozies.

Case in point, Ojai, California, home to Larry Hagman, who rose to fame as "Master" on the *I Dream of Jeanie* TV show and whose career peaked by getting shot as the nefarious J.R. Ewing on the prime time soap opera, *Dallas*. There was no way Hagman and his high-end neighbors were going to look out the windows of their McMansions and see a big, white radar eyeball staring back at them, so they circled the wagons. The conflagration came to a head on the Montel Williams Show, and I was in the studio audience with my boss from Washington, Tim Tomastik.

In this corner, representing the government, and its ill-advised massive radar tower that's going to give everyone cancer is Dr. Elbert "Joe" Friday, director of the National Weather Service.

"Boooooooooooooo."

And appearing on behalf of the God-fearing people of Ojai who just want to be left alone by the big, bad government, is television superstar and neighborhood hero, Larry "J.R." Hagman.

"Yaaaay!

It was painfully clear which side Montel was on and Joe Friday shot occasional glares at Tim Tomastik for arranging such a lopsided confrontation. Larry challenged the Washington bureaucrat to prove the radar won't give everyone cancer.

"We can prove it's safer than the TV the people at home are watching this on," Joe argued.

"Balderdash," Hagman retorted. "Radar causes cancer."

To prove Larry's point, Montel brought on his next guest, an odd looking fellow who, if you pictured an obsessed scientist toiling in a secret lab all day, you'd picture him, the type who wears tinfoil under his hat to ward off the evil rays the government uses for mind control.

"No doubt about it, radar causes cancer," he said as he slammed down a stack of documents that would somehow prove his point. Our goose was pretty much cooked, but the Hagman-Williams team had one more rabbit in their hat.

Next up was a young lady with cancer. She didn't know exactly how she got it, but she did live next to a radar tower once and that was probably it.

Joe Friday was mortified and the studio audience bordered on lynch mob. At the commercial break, Tim confronted the producer. "You set us up you bastard," he yelled as two security guards escorted him off the set.

A few years later, the Enquirer reported that Hagman's liver was shot from years of hard drinking and he was in line for a transplant. I wondered why he didn't blame that on radar too.

The next stop on the angry community tour found me laughing harder than I ever laughed in my entire life, the kind where milk comes out of your nose when you were a kid.

Our construction crew was stopped cold by protesters on the Helderberg Escarpment, a high hill overlooking Albany, the capital of New York, where we were trying to build one of our new radars. Washington dispatched a team and I was to accompany them to help soothe the natives. Out on the escarpment, we drove up a narrow dirt road and had no choice but to stop behind the line of trucks that were carrying the carefully wrapped pieces of the evil contraption. At the top, we squared off with the citizenry and the dialogue went something like this:

"We're from the government and we're here to help," said our main guy, Caldwell.

"If you want to help, turn your trucks around and get the hell out of here," countered the ringleader.

"We're the federal government and you have no power to stop us."

"We're not moving."

"We can make you move."

"How are you going to do that?"

"We'll call the Sheriff."

"I'll save you the trouble."

The man punched into his cell phone as both sides scuffed the earth with their shoes.

"Hello dad..."

"I think we should vamoose," I whispered.

Like cowboys backing away from a rattlesnake, we eased toward our car and got the hell out of there.

"We'll be back," Caldwell said, shaking his fist at no one but us.

But this wasn't what had me laughing.

We repaired to the local diner to plot our next move. It was here that I brought up the conversation we had with a lady and her son up on the escarpment. She had just moved from California, Larry Hagman's neighborhood in Ojai to be exact, to get away from the radar we were trying to build there. She moved, she said, because she wanted to have grandchildren and if they put up the radar her son's precious reproductive equipment would be zapped and he would be unable to reproduce. And now, she's moved clear across the country only to find herself in the same predicament. The team looked over to the son who, we were quick to conclude, wasn't going to get too far in the romance department anyway with his bald head, beer gut, and coke bottle glasses.

"I can tell you one thing," Caldwell blurted. "That lady ain't getting no grandchildren and it ain't because of our damned radar." Maybe it was because we were at the end of a long day, or maybe because I was holding in all of the tension from up on the escarpment, but Caldwell's image of that poor grandchild-less mother and her dorky son caused me to embark on a laugh so deep, my face cramped and my stomach hurt the next day.

Back at the office I figured out a way to win over the Helderberg skeptics. When driving up the dirt road, I noticed two things: Branches scraped against the car on either side and one of the vehicles parked at the top was a landscape company truck. It belonged to the ringleader.

"Would you be interested in a contract to keep the road clear?" I asked him. To this day, I bet the government is still paying him the money.

CHAPTER 19

THE CHRISTMAS MIRACLE

"Bob, I like hanging out with you and listening to your stories, but everything's so damn gory and depressing," said Harvard one rainy night. "Don't you have anything with a happy ending?"

"As a matter of fact, I do," I replied and told him the story of *The Christmas Miracle*.

One holiday season, my friend The Took and I decided to sell Christmas trees for some extra cash. We secured a lot on a busy road in Flanders complete with a 55 gallon drum to make a cozy fire that we could huddle around and keep warm. Better yet, we had a box truck and trailer to drive upstate to buy the trees cheap and bring them down to Long Island to make our killing. What could go wrong?

The trip north to Lake Placid was uneventful, our obedient trailer following behind. We would stay overnight and hit the tree farm a few miles south of the Canadian border in the morning. A single Christmas tree is relatively light, maybe 30 pounds plump from the farm. But when 200 of them gang up on you, you're looking at three tons. The farmhands were either as clueless as we were or devious since they loaded up the trailer with the bulk of the trees making it much heavier than the few dozen they tossed in the back of the truck. We pulled out with quite an unbalanced load, the trailer tires squashed from the burden.

On Interstate 87 outside Schroon Lake in the heart of the Adirondacks, one of the trailer tires couldn't take it anymore and blew out causing the trailer to sway wildly. The overweight trailer fish-tailed the truck and our hearts were in our throats as The Took wrestled us to the apron.

"Fuck! Flat tire."

Rooting around the cab, The Took could not find the jack, which didn't matter anyway, because we carried no spare. Standing there on the side of the road in the middle of nowhere we made an amazing discovery: down below on the service road was a gas station with a gleaming new wrecker. We bolted down to it and the man said he wasn't very busy and could come up and give it a look. Luck was back in our corner as the tow truck guy was not only able to jack up the trailer and remove the flat, but also replace both tires with brand new ones in stock from the service station.

We were back on our way, but not before throwing off every single tree to the side of the road and repacking them in a more balanced manner. People driving by must have thought we were nuts. Through the rest of the trip, over the various bridges and winter potholes of New York City, 315 miles in all, our eyes were glued to the rearview mirrors to watch those whirling black donuts roll our precious cargo home.

The next day was a flurry of activity at the Christmas tree lot with the two entrepreneurs making signs and stands for our fragrant wares. We offered gorgeous balsam firs, scotch pines, and spruces, not to mention pine roping and wreaths. After a long day and a couple of happy customers, we were settling around our warm barrel when we heard a couple of pops like fire crackers going off. We didn't think much of it until a few minutes later when police descended like locusts on the auto body shop across the street. The owner was shot dead, the assailant vanishing into the night. Two detectives stepped past the yellow crime scene tape to question us.

"Did you see anyone with a gun?"

"No."

"Did you see anyone across the street?"

"No."

"Did you see anything suspicious?"

"No."

They looked at us suspiciously.

"How is it that someone gets shot right across the street and you didn't see anything?"

"Well, we did hear it."

"You heard it! What did you hear?"

"We heard the shots. Sounded like firecrackers."

"How many shots?" the interrogation continued.

"Three," we said in harmony."

"What did you see after that?"

"Nothing. We thought it was a couple of firecrackers."

The detectives looked at each other and shook their heads.

The police set up a roadblock and were scrutinizing every driver passing through. Some were directed into our parking lot for further questioning. Needless to say, Christmas tree sales slowed to a crawl, though one state trooper came back with his pickup and bought one.

The next day we were back in business, though people seemed hesitant to stop with all the police tape still fluttering in the breeze. I was warming my hands by the fire when The Took snuck up behind me and popped a plastic bag by my head. It scared the crap out of me and I chased after him like a cat and mouse through the trees. Night started to fall and our Charlie Brown Christmas lot, lit up by a couple of strings of light bulbs, looked kind of nice. We didn't have any sales on the day, but it sure smelled good.

Suddenly, we heard a few more explosions, this time a little further down the street. I looked at The Took with an expression that wondered, "What-the-fuck-was-that?"

Sure enough, it was gunshots and the police closed off the street once again. Same two dicks paid us a visit.

"No."

"No."

"No."

"Yup, we heard it."

"We were hoping they were just fire crackers."

"Three," we said in harmony."

"Flanders Under Siege From Christmas Sniper," the newspapers rang out the next morning. On consecutive nights, two men were shot. The first was killed by a small caliber rifle, shot in the head. The gunman even killed his dog. The second had his two middle fingers blown off by a shotgun blast as he sat watching TV with his hands clasped behind his head. Motorists sped by the tree lot, not even looking our way.

Admittedly, the part of Flanders where we set up shop was no Marvin Gardens. It's primarily a minority area and before the Christmas Sniper struck, the people were very friendly to us. We delivered a few trees and even received tips from customers who appeared barely able to afford it. Right away, the chatter turned to drugs and it was assumed that the victims were wrapped up in something unsavory. The police were playing it close to the vest and the greater Flanders area took to the mattresses. Still, we stayed at the tree farm to guard against the looting and mayhem we were certain would occur had we left our post.

On the third day of our ill-fated enterprise, we had only a single visitor: a salesman offering quickie pistol licenses and some cheap handguns. We politely said no, not divulging the fact we already had some firepower: a 12-gauge shotgun and a .22 rifle stashed under the wreaths.

Just after sunset, The Took and I heard a rustling in the bushes across the street and we sidled over to our weapons. We watched as a man emerged with camouflage paint on his face and grass sticking out of his clothes.

"Police," he shouted, "It's okay." He's lucky we didn't shoot him.

He told us the area was being staked out and not to worry. When he suggested that we close up shop, we hightailed it out of there thinking the trees were in good hands for the evening.

The morning paper gave us another fright: "Christmas Sniper Strikes Again!" This time the target was shot through the window of his house shortly after he answered a knock on the door with nobody there. He was wounded in the shoulder. The police said the weapon was the same shotgun fired the night before. Our new advertising campaign, "Christmas Trees ½ Price," drew zero customers and we called it quits early.

Sometimes you expect bad news and the next morning paper confirmed our intuition: "Sniper Rampage Continues; Fourth Man Shot." The gunman had another busy night and our dream of extra cash for the holidays evaporated with the headlines. This time he shot a man in the jaw with a .22-caliber bullet as he sat in his home.

While we skulked in the shadows of our idle trees, the gunman got bolder. He called the police and said the cops were crooked and his victims were drug dealers who had it coming. The police responded by saying there was no evidence the shootings were drug related and the gunman was only trying to mislead the authorities.

Great comfort in that, we thought.

After the fourth incident, the sniper took a recess, but the community remained on edge. Terror kept the buyers away. Our misfortune meant a bonanza for our friends and family who were the recipients of ridiculously cheap trees, okay, free, which we even delivered, and we donated a few to the Moriches Bay Historical Society thrift sale.

It had been 17 days since the sniper last struck and on Christmas Eve, Flanders wouldn't be denied a happy holiday. They came out in force and bought up everything we had left.

"Was that the miracle?" Harvard asked.

"No. Just hold your horses."

CHAPTER 20

THE COMMANDO

It wasn't until the late hours of New Year's Eve that the sniper would return. After calling in a bogus accident report, he blasted out the emergency lights of the responding officer's patrol car and disappeared. Flanders went back into panic mode and kicked off the year in fear.

In late January, police were alerted to a cache of guns hidden in a car and were able to trace them to the shootings. Six days later, 21-year-old Yusef Abdullah Rahman was arrested as the Christmas Sniper.

Fascinated with guns since he was a little kid, Rahman fancied himself as a commando. Wearing a bullet-proof vest and military-like clothing, he rode around on a bicycle looking for people to shoot. In a confession to the police, the sniper said he started playing army combat games when he was 6 years old and bought his first real gun at 14. He killed someone four years later.

"It appears that he enjoyed killing," said Timothy Mazzei, deputy chief of the district attorney's homicide bureau. "He got his kicks out of playing army and shooting people." The chief of police called him "a bad boy."

Rahman liked to practice combat training maneuvers and the day we heard his first shots, he said he was crawling around the woods when he encountered a dog, which he shot. He said he then saw the dog's owner, and shot him. His defense lawyer contended that he was suffering from the delusions of a paranoid schizophrenic and believed he was on a military combat mission with Tall Man, Radio Man, Blaster and five other soldiers. He was part of a secret government task force assigned to special missions and got his orders over a military radio.

We also learned he was facing extradition to Missouri where, as Joseph Davis, he was wanted for murder.

"He wanted to kill all the drug dealers in Kansas City," a police sergeant said, and was suspected of an execution-style killing of a youth. He lived for about two years in a shack in the woods and detectives knew him as "Rambo." He also was facing auto theft charges and was wanted for questioning in four other fatal shootings.

"I don't know why I shot this man," Mr. Rahman said describing the third attack. "I just wanted to shoot someone."

Rahman's insanity defense didn't hold up and he was sentenced to 42 years to life.

The Took and I remain utterly amazed that the sniper didn't pick off the easiest of his potential targets—two hustlers huddled around a fire in an open lot trying to sell Christmas trees.

"For Christ's sake," Harvard said after sitting there patiently. "That's not a happy ending."

"What do you mean?"

Four guys and a dog got shot, and one guy died. What kind of miracle is that?"

"The miracle is we didn't get shot."

CHAPTER 21

EGYPTAIR

"Alright Mr. Story Teller, I have time for one more," Sandy said, fidgeting with her straw. "What else you got?"

"It was a dark and stormy night," I started.

"Come on, get serious."

It really was a lousy night and I was holed up in a rickety old Howard Johnson hotel off Narragansett Bay in Rhode Island. The wind was blowing so hard it was rattling the doors of the rooms and I couldn't sleep. I was there for another crash: EgyptAir Flight 990 disappeared into the Atlantic 60 miles south of Nantucket and the NOAA Ship Whiting was on the scene looking for the pieces.

Thank God I'm not out there tonight, I thought, practically tasting the purple milkshake I hurled during the Flight 800 mission.

My immediate concern was a peaceful night's sleep and I knew I would be miserable at the command center if I was dragging ass all day. So I employed a solution learned when I was living in the dorms at Oswego College. If you jam enough coins in the crack of someone's door, the pressure on the bolt keeps them from unlocking it and they're trapped. More than one co-ed was late for class thanks to getting "pennied." So I crept out into the hall with a handful of change and was able to silence the doors that were making the racket.

Flight 990 created an international stir between Egypt and America with each country conducting their own investigations. Egypt concluded it was mechanical error and fixed the blame on the Boeing Corp for the 767's demise. But the U.S. came up with a more sinister cause, keying in on a phrase repeated by a relief pilot eleven times as the plane went down.

The flight from New York to Cairo had two sets of pilots: the first pair handling the takeoff and half of the flight and the second pair taking over the rest of the way. Just after the plane lifted off, a pilot from the second crew, Gameel Al-Batouti, ordered the younger co-pilot out of his chair and flew the plane with the first pilot. Later, when he stepped out for a bathroom break, Al-Batouti promptly put the plane into a nose dive shouting, "Tawakkalt ala Allah," I rely on God.

The flight recorder picks up the action:

"What's happening, Gameel? What's happening?" the first pilot shouts as he rushes back in.

"Tawakkalt ala Allah" Al-Batouti responds as he shuts off the fuel to both engines.

"What is this? Did you shut the engines?" the first pilot asks, grabbing the controls. "Pull with me! Pull with me!"

"Tawakkalt ala Allah."

Flight 990 soared back up to 24,000 feet and then broke apart from the stress.

It turns out Al-Batouti was under fire for sexual misconduct, including exposing himself to teenage girls, propositioning hotel maids and stalking female guests. His boss, Hatem Rushdy, the chief of EgyptAir's Boeing 767 pilot group, had reprimanded him and told him Flight 990 would be his last transatlantic route. Rushdy was the first pilot on the doomed plane. According to a former EgyptAir pilot in the Los Angeles Times, Al-Batouti's attitude was, "This is the last flight for you too." A high-ranking U.S. investigator agreed: "It was more revenge against Rushdy than just a suicide." Everyone aboard, 217 souls, lost their lives.

CHAPTER 22

FREE TO FLY

John F. Kennedy, Jr. strode up to his Piper Saratoga airplane as commander of the world. His magazine on politics and society, George, was a sensation and he was eyed as heir apparent to the White House—if he wanted it.

Why drive all the way to Massachusetts when we can just hop in my plane and fly? the aviator thought to himself.

Was he nervous about taking off that night? Maybe. He had his pilot's license for only a year and his plane was powerful and fast. John limped from an ankle injury, hurt while hang gliding the previous month, and perhaps he was taking something for the pain. Did he possess all his faculties?

Everything checked out on the six-seater and he gallantly ushered in his precious cargo. He was as proud as a teenager driving his first car to freedom. Maybe Carolyn and Lauren had second thoughts, but this was John, a man of great confidence and gravitas. Surely, he would deliver them safely, first to Martha's Vineyard where he was to drop off his sister-in-law, and then to Hyannis Port for his cousin Rory Kennedy's wedding. Maybe Carolyn voiced her fears over flying and he overruled them. Or maybe Sandy was right: John John was the one with second thoughts.

The first leg of the journey would take them from the Essex County Airport in New Jersey to Martha's Vineyard, a 200-mile jaunt. The flight would be over water—the Long Island Sound and then the Atlantic. John would be flying visually, not yet trusting of his instruments.

Crossing the sound, the haze blinded John like two hands over his face. Gone were the familiar lights of Connecticut and Long Island. The flier had no reference points and couldn't see where he was going. But his compass pointed east and he soldiered on.

CHAPTER 23

THE LONGEST NIGHT

"Your timing couldn't be better," said the captain of the Rude, the same ship that located the wreckage of Flight 800. "I think we found him." My Washington bosses felt the John F. Kennedy, Jr. mission would be better served if their ace PR man was at the scene and I was escorted to the NOAA ship by a Coast Guard patrol boat at nightfall.

Scrolling across the screen came an eerie presence I knew not to be found in nature: a rectangular shape with straight edges. The next few minutes were a blur of activity ending when a Navy boat dropped a buoy on the exact spot. We were ordered to stand away and it was decided for the night I would be transferred to berth aboard the Whiting, a larger NOAA vessel also on the scene. Their mission complete, most of the Whiting's crew had turned in for the night and after I was shown my bunk and a small dining area with a little television, I was left to fend for myself.

"Help yourself," said the mate as he gestured at a tray of chips and wrinkled fruit, a sparse offering that would be my dinner. I didn't look forward to spending the night on the water.

Exhausted, I found my way along the steel corridors back to my bunk and tried to sleep, the cramped quarters closing in around me. The voice of the ship, an inescapable hum, droned on my weary consciousness and the damp air weighed down on me like the oily, long-ago smell of accident scenes. The magic of my last Dramamine ebbed from my system and the walls of my sarcophagus kept spinning even after I squinted my eyes shut.

Giving up on sleep, I wound my way back to the mess area and turned on the TV, its rabbit ears had tin foil on them to grab the only channel to be had at sea. The 11 o'clock news had just begun. "Hope is slowly giving way to heartache at the Kennedy compound as chances dim for the safe arrival of John F. Kennedy, Jr.," the broadcaster intoned through the static. "Lost somewhere over the Atlantic during a flight from a small airport in New Jersey, Kennedy's plane apparently did not complete it intended route."

Then the images began. The widow, veiled in black, bends to whisper in a small boy's ear. He snaps to attention and smartly salutes his fallen father. The fuzzy screen shows the boy peering out from behind the Oval Office desk, a playful imp at the feet of the most powerful man in the world. He dances with his sister, their feet skimming the rug as the president claps in sheer delight. Steering a motorboat, his little head barely peers over the wheel. And then, in full manhood, John John emerges from the surf, his bare chest sculpted, to glaze the eyes of women everywhere. The Adonis poses with starlets, the envy of the world. The scion of Camelot speaks at the Democrat convention, a president to be.

Head spinning and stomach churning, I slump into the hard chair. There's John on his bicycle, dodging the paparazzi, and him again, announcing his new magazine, supermodel Cindy Crawford appearing as George Washington on the glossy cover. He lounges on yachts off stunning Greek isles, cavorts with superstars and then, spitting his silver spoon at a doubting public, graduates from the New York University School of Law and takes a job with the Manhattan district attorney, passing the bar exam after three celebrated tries.

John had the privileges of a prince—fame, fortune, good looks, and the ability to do anything he wanted. Would he have given it all up to have his father back?

Back in my bunk, the questions closed in. Was he warned about the haze? Why didn't he turn on his transponder so air traffic control would know where he was? Or did he feel invincible and like everything else, could easily handle anything his complicated, glorious life threw his way?

CHAPTER 24

THE CRASH

In the inky cockpit, Carolyn knew something was wrong. The engine wailed and the tilt of the plane seemed unnatural, even though their minds told them they were going straight. John John was agitated, his head darted about and his hands, stark white, strangled the yoke.

Look at the bubble, look at the bubble, my nightmare wrenched me awake. *For God's sake, John, why don't you just look at the bubble?*

The black haze hiding his visual guideposts, the pilot could not orient himself. Up was down and down was up. He thought he was flying straight, but he was tilted, and losing altitude.

Look at the bubble!

The cockpit was chaos.

"Shut up, just shut up," John yelled, the engine screaming through the terrible night.

The wings, John, they're not level. For God's sake, look at the bubble!

The compass spun from east to north, 2,000 feet.

John's training abandoned him, his lack of experience haunted.

"We're going to die," a voice sobbed, though John didn't know whose.

"Shut up, shut up!"

West, south, the compass was of no use, 1,000 feet. John pulled on the yoke.

Goddammit John, the bubble is crooked, your wings are not level!

Pulling back on the yoke with level wings will cause your plane to rise, just like Gruff would do to put you into a huge loop. But John was tilted and as he pulled back, he put his Piper Saratoga into long, drawn-out turn.

The altimeter plummeted: 500, 250.

"What is happening?"

John was in a death spiral. Unable—or unwilling—to believe the instruments and relying on instinct which, in his tragic case, was failing him. His wings were tilted and he was pulling back on the yoke, hastening his path to the sea.

Chapter 25

TURNING AWAY

The Whiting rolled ever so slightly as I climbed down to the Coast Guard boat that would take me back to solid ground. I was pale and sick. We bobbed within earshot of the Navy's dreary, gray ship, a thin line from its crane reaching into the water. I held a camera in my hand. Up from the depths came the ghastly image: John F. Kennedy, Jr.'s Piper Saratoga, wings shorn, twisted beyond recognition. For me, death would have been a welcome relief. The wreckage was quickly surrounded by the living and mercifully, my transport turned and sped away. I didn't take any pictures.

CHAPTER 26

THE TALKER HITS THE JACKPOT

The Talker, Danny Pelosi, found himself one autumn night at the mansion of Ted Ammon, a millionaire financier. The gabled, English-style home was part of the exclusive enclave of East Hampton, a far cry from our working-class hamlet of Center Moriches. Danny had gained the acquaintance of Ammon's wife, Generosa, when she was in the throes of divorce from her investment banker husband. He was a contractor at her multi-million dollar apartment renovation in Manhattan and they hit it off from word one. Danny described it as winning the Lotto. Generosa thought Ted had a woman on the side and was hiding his money to throw off the settlement talks. If it was her plan to torment her husband by hooking up with his polar opposite she couldn't have picked a better candidate. While Ted was accomplished and rich, Danny was bankrupt and said things like "yous guys." While Ted was chairman of Jazz at Lincoln Center and skirted the globe in private jets, Danny held court in bars and spent time in jail for drunken driving. Generosa was the princess and the smooth talker with the tool belt would do whatever she said.

With Generosa, Danny finally got to live like he always thought he should. He accompanied her to New York's finest places and could be seen tooling around the Hamptons in the tycoon's Porsche. He befriended Ammon's two adopted twins, Alexa and Grego, and served as a dull knife driven by Generosa into Ted Ammon's back. Danny's clothes got better and, if it was any consolation, we saw him less and less.

Around noon one day, the news tore through the Sports Page like a tornado: Ted Ammon was found bludgeoned to death in the bedroom of his East Hampton estate.

"Danny did it."

"No way."

"Killed him for the money."

At the time of the murder, the divorce settlement had not been finalized and Generosa was in line for the bulk of Ted's multi-million dollar estate.

"Makes all the sense in the world," Harvard surmised. "Danny knocked him off so Generosa would get all the money. You don't have to be a brain surgeon to figure that one out."

But it took the police a while to build their case and Danny sightings became our obsession.

"I saw him going into the bakery with Generosa and the kids," Sandy reported.

"I spotted him in the bay driving a brand new boat," Big Daddy said.

"Impossible," countered the barkeep. "He's living in London on Ted's country estate."

One place he didn't go was the Sports Page Bar and Restaurant.

And then the sightings became more frequent. "Danny's moved back to Center Moriches," Harvard sang out, "and he's got Generosa with him."

"They got married," Sandy announced.

"Isn't that a little too obvious?" Harvard shot back.

"It's true. Danny got his divorce and married her the next day."

"Good God!"

I didn't think Danny did it. He was a lot of things, bullshit artist being his most endearing trait, but murderer? I didn't think he had it in him.

"Don't you get it," Harvard tried to set me straight. "Generosa's a real operator. She lined up Danny like a pro. Showered him with money and glitz. And when the time came, he knew what he had to do."

"So he went out to East Hampton and knocked off the husband just like that." Everyone looked at me like I was an idiot. "It seems too perfect. I mean, what are we in freaking Hollywood? Stuff like that just doesn't happen around here. And really, is Danny that stupid?"

"Yup."

"You bet."

"Did it for the money."

My disgusted face scanned the crowd. In the stagnant air of the gin mill, the news channels blared the details of the case and Danny's face looked out from every paper scattered on the bar.

"Son of a bitch. Maybe he did."

As the soap opera wore on, we were treated to another tidbit:

"Generosa's dead."

"What?"

"And that's not even the half of it," Sandy said, slapping the day's paper on the bar. "Check this out."

A forlorn Danny was pictured at their favorite haunt, the Stanhope Hotel lounge in Manhattan, an urn containing Generosa's ashes at his side. He had called the New York Post to make sure they knew he was there.

"I know she would have wanted it this way," Sandy read from the paper. "I think I'm gonna puke."

CHAPTER 27

DID HE DO IT?

There was one lady The Talker could not charm: Janet Albertson, the petite but potent, assistant district attorney. While it sure looked like Danny killed the millionaire, it was Albertson who had to prove it in a court of law. She came out with guns blazing.

First, she labored over crime scene photos of the beaten body and blood stains. Ted put up quite a struggle, but in the end laid there dead, naked, and covered in his own blood. "What happened to Ted Ammon could have killed three men, yet alone one," Albertson said. "That's how brutal this homicide was."

She asked the obvious: Did Danny have a motive? Absolutely. He did it for the money.

Was Danny familiar with the East Hampton manse? For sure. He was there plenty of times.

Did Danny have a heart of stone? Yup. Just look how he dumped his wife and kids when Generosa came along.

And then there was the matter of the surveillance system. Generosa had her Danny, but she wasn't about to let Ted slip from her grasp. She directed Danny to install a surveillance system in the East Hampton house so she could lord over it. From a computer, anywhere in the world, Generosa could keep tabs on Ted.

Danny was familiar with the surveillance system, the bulldog prosecutor told the jury. He knew how to remove the hard drive so there would be no record of that fatal night. Conveniently, the hard drive was nowhere to be found. Danny knew how to cover his tracks.

"If someone wanted to get rid of something you never wanted to be found, what would you do?" was the question Danny posed to his father at a family wedding the day Ted's body was found. This little piece of condemning information wasn't just hearsay. It came from Danny's father himself, in testimony for the prosecution.

"His own dad?" Harvard exclaimed to the barfly jury. "His own dad testifying against him? Now that's rough."

Robert Pelosi was cross examined by Danny's lawyer, famed Manhattan criminal defense attorney Gerry Shargel, best known for springing mobster John Gotti, the Teflon Don.

"Do you hate your son?" Shargel asked the senior Pelosi.

"No, I love him."

The defense admitted into evidence letters between the two. Through Danny's wayward years, drunken driving arrests, stints in jail, his father wanted him to grow up, be more responsible. But that never happened and Mr. Pelosi disowned his son, writing he no longer wanted Danny's childhood possessions—his old baseball cap, report cards—in his home. Danny wrote back pleading for forgiveness.

"Danny disappointed me," the father told the court. "He disgraced the name Pelosi—a very proud name."

Did he blame Danny for the death of his favorite son, respectable New York City police officer Jimbo Pelosi, who died suddenly during the throes of the scandal?

"I love you, Danny, whether you know it or not," the father spoke not to the lawyer, but to the defendant.

"Did you break his nose once?" Shargel bored in.

"Shame on you," the father yelled across the courtroom. "I broke your nose?"

"You couldn't!"

"What does that mean?"

"You know what I mean."

As his father stepped down from the stand, Danny muttered within earshot of the jury: "I hate him."

"I hate him too," said Sandy.

Next up for the prosecution was Tracey Riebenfeld, a petite brunette billed as Danny's girlfriend.

"When the hell did he have time for her?" Sandy asked out loud.

It seems that a few months after Ted's murder, Danny had this to say to Tracey: "I bashed his fucking brains in, and he cried like a bitch and he begged for his life."

"Why in hell would he tell her that?" Sandy looked around the bar.

Tracey told the jury that when she asked why he did it, Danny pounded his chest and said, "Because I have a monster in me!"

"Oh brother."

The defense hammered back, depicting Riebenfeld as a jilted lover looking for revenge because Danny dumped her.

"That's ridiculous." Riebenfeld retorted. "Do you think it's pleasurable for me to sit here?"

"Ridiculous, I'll say," Sandy yelled out. "Danny never loved her."

Batting next for the people was James Nicolino, another contractor who worked on Generosa's Manhattan pad. A year before, Danny told him he was going to kill Ted and marry Generosa. But the defense quickly brushed that one back claiming Nicolino was prejudiced because Pelosi had an affair with his wife.

"What the fuck?" Sandy exclaimed.

Next on the agenda was Clayton Moultrie, a fellow inmate of Danny's who told the jury Danny admitted the whole thing to him in a jailhouse confession.

"Either the DA has a magic wand or Danny just doesn't know when to keep his mouth shut," Harvard stated the obvious.

Not long after Moultrie hammered his nail into Danny's coffin, he was released from jail—and promptly re-arrested for robbing a convenience store with an ice pick.

Danny made sure his three kids were not in court to witness the daily spectacle, but he did have one special guest: his new fiancée, Jennifer Zolnowski. Whenever he got the chance, he'd turn his head over his shoulder and blow kisses to the buxom blond.

"You gotta hand it to him," Harvard said. "Getting engaged while defending a murder rap. You can't make this stuff up."

"What a slut," retorted Sandy.

Finally there was the worker who said Danny had a new stun gun delivered to the Manhattan job and was chasing the workers around with it. He offered them a hundred bucks a pop if he could zap them.

"That's Danny for you."

Experts from each side argued whether those were really zap marks on Ted's body.

Danny summed it up to everyone within earshot: "They ain't got no goddamn case against me. If they had a murder case, they wouldn't use this bullshit."

"He didn't do it," Sandy startled the bar. "Just listen to the defense. Danny was with a friend all night. He has an alibi. And what about Ted's call to his girlfriend? Someone scared him at the gay beach he was at. Maybe he was followed home. Maybe he really is a faggot and things got out of hand with someone he met."

The defense planted every imaginable doubt. Shargel put Ted's girlfriend on the stand and got her to say the tycoon would never have left his clothes piled in a heap on the floor. He was too "fastidious" to do that, Shargel said, implying Ted was gay. It could have been a quick romp in the hay with someone he met. Maybe the encounter turned violent.

Ted didn't get rich without making enemies, the defense pressed on. These "Master of the Universe" types ruffle feathers. You don't make millions taking over companies without somebody wanting to kill you.

And then there was the business partner who flew from New York to East Hampton in a helicopter because he was worried about Ted. After he discovered the body, he fed the dog and erased the messages on Ted's phone before calling the police.

The case was circumstantial with no direct evidence. Danny had a fighting chance.

Chapter 28

THE TALKER KEEPS TALKING

Grinning as if he was announcing the arrival of his first born, Danny turned to the gallery as his defense rested. "I'm going to testify!"

The courtroom buzzed like somebody struck the hive. Shargel was stunned and the judge asked aloud, "Are you kidding?"

Albertson rubbed her hands. "This is too good to be true."

The prosecution's case rested on what Danny supposedly said to others and now, the accused was going to take the stand to tell everyone himself.

"He's out of his mind," Harvard announced.

"Albertson will cut him to pieces," Big Daddy piled on.

"Do you think they'll believe him?" wondered Sandy.

It had to be the performance of his life and The Talker just wasn't up to the task. The gambit boiled down to Danny denying he killed Ted Ammon and whether or not the jury would believe him. Danny looked nervous as hell, and at one point, his lawyer asked him if he wanted some water. "I need a drink," was Danny's response.

"You've told many boastful stories in your life, haven't you?" Shargel asked.

"Yes I have." Danny answered proudly.

"You could say you are a bullshitter, right?"

"Absolutely."

"There you have it," Sandy retorted. "Right from the horse's mouth. All the crap he told everybody—all bullshit."

Albertson asked the final question: "Are you bullshitting the jury now, Mr. Pelosi?"

"No, I am not."

"Guilty," Harvard exclaimed.

"Guilty as sin," concluded Big Daddy.

We all looked at Sandy. "What a moron."

CHAPTER 29

GENEROSA'S MONEY

It took three days for the jury to decide if they believed Danny. Deliberating over the weekend, the verdict was delivered on a Monday: Guilty. Soon after, The Talker was sentenced to the maximum penalty of 25 years to life.

"Got what he deserved."

"Shouldn't have taken the stand."

"What a fucking idiot."

After the dust settled, it was Big Daddy who illuminated me at the bar one hazy night:

"Danny didn't set out to kill Ted Ammon for the money—Generosa was going to get plenty of that in the settlement. Danny killed Ted at the mansion that night because he was there with Sandy and Ted caught them. Ted threatened to tell Generosa and the gravy train would have ground to a halt. Danny didn't kill Ted for Ted's money," Big Daddy concluded. "He killed him for Generosa's."

Chapter 30

DANNY COMES CLEAN

After seven years rotting at the Great Meadow Correctional Facility in upstate New York, Danny Pelosi enlisted Cynthia McFadden of WABC's 20/20 to set the record straight. He was going to come clean on what happened the night Ted Ammon was murdered and lead her to evidence that would expose the real killer.

"The bottom line is that I did not kill Ted Ammon. I never did," Danny told McFadden in the opening segment, an armed guard standing not far behind them. "Generosa did not kill Ted Ammon. She had him killed."

According to Danny, Generosa was incensed because she thought Ted fathered a baby with another woman. "She wanted revenge because of that baby," Danny explained. "She went berserk. Out of this world. Insane. White hatred, psycho killer," he said, waving his arms for emphasis.

"Generosa came to my job one day and offered fifty thousand dollars to have her husband beat, beaten up. That's what she wanted. I brought it to other people. I said, 'Hey man, my girlfriend's offering fifty thousand dollars. Do you want to tune up her husband?' I got regular guys working for me. Fifty thousand dollars to throw somebody a beating. I'm sorry, everybody was interested on the job."

Danny said one of his workers, Chris Parrino, took her up on the offer.

"You're coming here, Chris," Danny pronounced on national television, banging on a jailhouse table. "I'm making sure you come here."

"Why would she need Chris when she's got you?" McFadden asked.

"Honest to God," he answered, "she didn't need Chris. I had no problem with tuning him up. I really didn't. I was going to do it right there in the Stanhope. No problem. On me."

"Before you could do it, what happened?"

"I'd get violated on probation," Danny was quick to respond. "I was on probation for a DWI, okay? I was gonna get a year in jail for smacking this guy in the face. It was guaranteed that he was gonna call the cops and that's why Generosa stopped me."

Danny admitted to paying Parrino the balance of the $50,000 after Ted was killed, but argued: "I'm not innocent in the things that happened after the murder and this is why I never told my story."

McFadden narrates: "Danny Pelosi said he knows exactly what happened to Ted Ammon that night because of what Parrino and Generosa later told him and because the night of the murder, he watched some of it unfold on the laptop that could access the camera system."

"Ted Ammon was dressed when he answered the door and got jacked up against the wall."

"By Chris Parrino?"

"Not by Chris Parrino, by dumb and dumber, the two guys that Chris had do this with him, the two guys that Chris subcontracted the tune up to."

"Do you know their names?"

"No, I don't know their names. They didn't know that there were nine cameras installed in there. They had no idea. So they came in. They jacked Ted up. They tuned him up for an hour. They tuned him up until Chris and Generosa got out there."

"Who are you saying killed Ted Ammon?"

"Ted Ammon was killed by Christopher Parrino and he told me it was an accident. He told me he smacked him in the head with the piece and knocked him out—left him there knocked out. He must have bled to death. Generosa confirmed it."

After the trial, Parrino confessed to driving Danny to East Hampton that night and said he came out of the house with blood on him, telling him he had a fight with Ted Ammon. "I think he's dead," Parrino quoted Danny as saying. Parrino copped a plea for hindering the prosecution and was sentenced to six months.

"That night, did she want him dead?"

"According to the guys there? Yes, Generosa gave the order to finish him," Danny said with a smirk. "Generosa, til the day she died, said he got exactly what he deserved. Period."

To protect Generosa, Danny said he had to get rid of the security system hard drive.

"I took out that video unit Monday morning. Ted was already dead. Ted was dead for a whole day and a half when I went there."

From here, Danny led 20/20 on a goose chase to a canal in Lindenhurst where he said he threw the box containing the video that would exonerate him.

"I tell you where it is, go get it. Put a guy in the water. Take a stick. Let me out of here. I'll go get it. I'll bring you right to it. I'll jump in the water. I'll pull it out of the mud," Danny said to the camera.

Driving home his point, Danny added: "I am very intelligent. I am very, very intelligent. If I wanted Ted Ammon killed, I could have drove by him at any time and put one in his head. But I don't shoot people. I am not a killer. I'm a contractor. I'll take your body and I'll throw you down by a foundation and I'll throw some dirt over it. They'll never find you ever. I sure as shit ain't going to kill you where I had a camera system installed.

In a scene reminiscent of Geraldo Rivera opening Al Capone's vault and finding nothing, divers hit the water in the murky canal guided by a hand-drawn map supplied by Danny. He confirmed the spot over a cell phone patched through to Great Meadow. After eight hours, the divers came up with a muddy cash register, tires and an old bike. No black box. Danny was crushed.

"There's five more creeks there. It's there. I know it's there. Maybe you might be done diving, but I'm not," he promised McFadden.

"Isn't it possible that the story you told me about what happened that night is exactly what happened except for one thing, that you were in that room," she asked.

"I can't be in that room. I didn't do the murder. He was already dead."

"But you covered it up. Fair Enough?"

"Fair enough. After the murder, yes. Did I protect Generosa? Yes. I'm not guilty of murder. I'm guilty of being an idiot."

Pressed for real evidence to prove his case, Danny went on, "A jury convicted me in a trial that was treated like a circus. My trial was a joke."

Shown a picture of the two children whose lives he ripped to shreds, Danny responded, "If I could do it all over, I would have walked out of the 87th Street building right after I got my money and never spent another minute with her."

"In 2003 you told me that when you met Generosa you hit the jackpot," McFadden concluded her interview. "Is that how it looks now?"

"I fell in a cesspool," Danny said, defeated. "And the worst part is, it's my own fault."

BOOK II:
THE DREAM
INTERRUPTED

CHAPTER 31

JOHN JOHN LIVES

My life went on with its ever-increasing stress and it was my stomach, not my brain, that finally cried uncle. One more shot of booze or another morning with hot coffee being the first thing to enter my system and my gullet would have burst. An energetic young lady I knew said her entire personality was based on coffee and I'm sorry to say more often than not it was the caffeine that did the talking for me. The "ine" drugs are killers—nicotine, codeine, morphine—and the one that took control of me was the one that is offered everywhere like a glass of water. Caffeine is a tough habit to shake and when the craving got too much, and I must tell you if you don't already know, the craving never leaves you, I would jump up from whatever I was doing and go for a walk to ward it off. I'd bend and stretch and get the blood flowing and maybe my desire for the comforting liquid would pass and my stomach would get another rare day of healing.

It was on one such jaunt that I ran into Sandra.

"There's always something I wanted to ask you," she told me after a big smile and a "How the hell are you?"

She hit me with it right there on the sidewalk, something I always banished on the little yellow bus that drives away my cares when I can't sleep.

"What if John John didn't die?"

I scratched my foot on the ground and avoided eye contact.

She shoved my shoulder. "You can write the story. Tell everybody what would have happened, what could have been."

"I don't know," I mumbled, "I'm pretty busy with other things."

"You have the talent, the power. You can make John anything you want. Come on, admit it, you're were obsessed with the guy, know everything about him. Hell, you practically lived your life through him. Now's your chance to finish the story."

I scraped some weeds with my foot.

"One week. I'll give you one week. We can meet at the old Sports Page, the same place, and you better be there with something good."

"Okay, okay, I'll do it, but it won't just be about John. You're going to hear more about me, what happened in my life."

"That's fine. I guess you've had a life too."

"And the world's going to hear all about it."

I needed more work like I needed a third eye, but John took hold of me again and I couldn't drive him away on the little bus. Where I once plopped down in front of the TV to pass the time, I now sat before the keypad. Where I once let my mind wander through its moods and madness, I was now focused like a laser. I would bring John back to life and tell the story of what could have been.

CHAPTER 32

THE GAGES

In his airplane somewhere over the deep, dark Atlantic, John fixed his eyes on the altimeter and the spinning numbers shot a jolt of panic through his system.

I'm pulling back on the yoke, but why am I losing altitude?

In the inky darkness, nothing made sense. The whine of the engine drowned out the screams of his passengers and all John could do was stare at the dial: 1,000 feet, 900, 800. His body was pressed against the seat like he was on a carnival Tilt-a-Whirl and his head felt like it was wrapped in gauze. He was paralyzed with fear and confusion and resigned his life to freefall with the plane.

Then, like the peal of a distant ocean bell, faint at first and then louder and louder, he made out the voice of his instructor, the man who sat with him through his intense hours of learning to fly, to fly blindly without seeing, with instruments and nothing outside but darkness and inside a gleaming panel of instruments that told you everything you needed to know to get back home.

"Level, John! Fly it level," the voice pressed, a frantic admonition from his deep memory. "Come on, John, straighten your wings."

But I am flying level. I can feel it. What the hell are you talking about?

"The gages, John, they are the truth. Look at the gages."

He squinted his eyes and the lights on the panel came into focus.

What's this?

A gage on the dash struck him as grotesque and another wave of panic coursed through him. The cockpit felt straight, but the little wings under the glass were horribly wrong. His eyes flashed to the bubble. It was pegged to one side. John's plane was tilted and he was turning and he was pulling back on the controls. He was in a death spiral.

This can't be!

John's hands were numb from strangling the yoke.

"Relax, John, relax."

He took a deep breath and loosened his grip.

He let the yoke find its center. The bubble went to the middle and the engine calmed to a steady hum. The throbbing in his head subsided and though his world was still engulfed in a bank of fog, he could see the faint glitter of water rushing beneath him. The altimeter read 200 feet.

John's passengers were silent, the chaotic decent left them breathless. His plane was flying straight now and his body gladly embraced the new perspective. Easing back on the yoke, John pointed his Piper Saratoga skyward and began to climb. With each breath his mind cleared and the vital details of his instrument training crept back into his consciousness.

I can do this.

He flipped on the plane's transponder and immediately a voice came over the radio.

"Piper Saratoga, Boston TRACON, maintain your ascent to three thousand, acknowledge."

"Climbing to three thousand."

"You saved him," Sandra said at our familiar place at the bar, only now it had a different name and the people were different too. We didn't recognize a soul. "Now what are you going to have him do?"

"Run for president, naturally."

CHAPTER 33

THE GREAT DIVIDE

John Kennedy's first interview as editor of his new magazine, George, was with former Alabama Governor George Wallace, the segregationist who was shot and paralyzed by Arthur Bremmer, a man motivated not by politics, but a desire for fame. Wallace was running for president of the United States and Bremmer's five bullets left him confined to a wheelchair for the rest of his life. The man who once yelled, "Segregation now, segregation tomorrow, segregation forever," stood in stark contrast to the Kennedy vision, one of civil rights and fairness and equality for all. He was a stunning choice for John's first edition. The former lion of racism was pictured in a wheelchair, old and frail with dirty fingernails.

Wallace and the man whose father produced the Civil Rights Act remind us that the people of history are not some storybook creatures, but souls like the rest of us. As high as you climb and as low as you sink, whether you live, are crippled or die, all of us must grapple with life's circumstances and get measured by what we make of them.

In the early 1970's, it was terrifying to be a small white boy in Center Moriches, New York. The black community, still stinging from the assassination of Dr. Martin Luther King, refused to wait any longer for equality and race riots were a regular part of the evening news. At school a black boy made a white girl cry by pulling down her dress and a dance ended in disaster when someone got hit with a microphone stand. Suddenly, the kid sitting next to you in social studies hated you. One hot afternoon across the street at the Hills shopping center, a sea of black and white swelled in the parking lot, angry faces taunting one another. Cops circled the warring factions and the high school principal waded in. Our town thankfully was small enough that everyone knew everyone else and after a lot of huffing and puffing, they all went home. As a little kid, I didn't understand the hatred, though I do know I was scared to death. The next morning, I mixed up a batch of fake puke and dumped it on my bedroom floor because I was too afraid to go to school.

The day after President Kennedy's inauguration, a black Air Force veteran named James Meredith resolved to exercise his constitutional rights and applied to the all-white University of Mississippi. He wanted the school to treat black Americans like the rest of the citizenry. Meredith was from Kosciusko, a Mississippi town named for the Polish general, a friend of Thomas Jefferson who fought with the Continental Army during the American Revolution. Ironically, the men who fought an epic war for freedom were slaveholders themselves.

JFK's attorney general, his brother Robert, convinced a reluctant Governor Ross Barnett to let Meredith enroll and he became the first African-American student at Ole Miss. White students and segregationists celebrated his arrival by rioting at the Oxford campus.

The Kennedys called in 500 U.S. Marshals and supported them with Army troops and the National Guard. At the university gate, a general's staff car was mobbed and set on fire. They managed to get out and crawl 200 yards to safety, all the while being shot at by angry protesters. Unbeknownst to the president, Barnett had pulled the state police from the scene.

In the clash over the admittance of a black student to a white college, two people died and 160 marshals and 40 soldiers were wounded. Despite being harassed and ostracized, Meredith graduated with a degree in Political Science. He wrote to Robert Kennedy:

"I am a graduate of the University of Mississippi. For this I am proud of my country — the United States of America. The question always arises — was it worth the cost? ... I believe that I echo the feeling of most Americans when I say that 'no price is too high to pay for freedom of person, equality of opportunity, and human dignity."

In Center Moriches, blacks lived north of the railroad tracks and the whites lived south and we were thus segregated except in one place, our school. Despite the outside agitators and what we saw on TV, the kids knew one thing to be true: We sat in the same classrooms and played on the same teams and on the field, we were winners. The white kids passed the ball to the black kids and goals were scored. On the diamond, the ball went around the horn to blacks and whites alike and we won. Center Moriches produced champions as the races played together as one.

CHAPTER 34

OPRAH

Along with James Meredith another famous American, Oprah Winfrey, hailed from Kosciusko, Mississippi. It was from her 1996 interview with John John that we get a peek into his closely guarded persona. The Talk Show Queen started off by gushing, "He is here! Everything you ever thought, you ever heard, you ever read about John F. Kennedy, Jr., he is all that, and then some." He entered to a standing ovation and quipped to Oprah, "Wow, you do this every day?"

Asked about his privacy, John said, "I've got a little bit. I've got enough." Pressed by Oprah, he continued: "We're used to a certain degree of being watched and I think that you are aware of it, even if you're not consciously aware of it. And I understand that there is interest. It's given us both great opportunities so I can't complain too much," he said of himself and his sister. "Sometimes I wish it wasn't always that way, but then you wouldn't have invited me on your show."

Oprah asked John if there was anyone who intimidated him. "Yeah, you do," he said with a laugh.

John was there to promote his new magazine and shared a story about interviewing Iain Calder, founding editor of the National Enquirer, the tabloid that epitomized his hounding. John said he asked him, "How do you sleep at night?" to which Calder responded, "Very well. I'm a sound sleeper."

"The funny thing was," John told Oprah, "he called me up afterwards and said, 'You misquoted me. There's things in here I never said.'"

Of all the crap the National Enquirer printed about John John and his family over the years, its editor was the one to complain.

Oprah touched on John's political coming out party at the 1988 Democratic National Convention where he introduced his uncle, Senator Ted Kennedy, who was running to follow in his brother's footsteps as president of the United States. After a standing ovation lasting a full minute, John said to the crowd: "Over a quarter century ago my father stood before you to accept the nomination for the presidency of the United States. So many of you came into public service because of him. In a very real sense, because of you, he is with us still. And for that, I'm grateful to all of you."

CHAPTER 35

ASK NOT...

Growing up, famous sayings didn't mean much to me except one, the challenge President Kennedy made to his fellow Americans at his 1961 Inauguration: "Ask not what your country can do for you—ask what you can do for your country."

The president's words echoed in my head as I considered a decision that would set the course for the rest of my life. While I would have wanted to stay at Suffolk Life Newspapers, it was the publisher's policy to force out the experienced reporters so he could tap an endless new crop willing to work on the cheap. I was grappling over two career paths: head to Washington to pursue a life in government or New York City to work on Wall Street and chase the money. I chose public service and scheduled a trip to Washington to see what I could do.

The day before the trip, I got a call from my state senator, Ken LaValle, who I had asked for a letter of recommendation. "Why don't you come to work for me?" he said when I told him of my plans. Going from a newspaper reporter to working for a state senator was a nice leap forward and I accepted. A day later, a county legislator who I had also asked for a letter offered me a job as well. He represented the Hamptons and ended up hiring a local party hack who was blamed for the legislator's defeat in his reelection. I'm quite sure he would have won had he called me a day earlier.

The New York State Legislature was in session when I started with the Senator and my first three weeks on the job were in

Albany. I had a desk in the LOB, Legislative Office Building, a misfit modernistic structure in the midst of the historic Capitol. A tiny fish in a big pond, I was awed by the ornate senate chambers and the magnificent Capitol Building. Massive sandstone staircases led to the rooms where I was to go to meetings and more than once I stopped mid-step to admire the faces of Washington, Lincoln, and Grant carved into the rock. At night, I jogged up and down the Capitol steps to make the Romanesque building my own. The seat of New York government stood magnificent thanks to grandiose designs by megalomaniac politicians fueled by taxpayer dollars. Yet blocks away, poverty surrounded the opulence.

I spent my days researching bills sponsored by the Senator and writing press releases to keep the folks informed back home. The most important item was the Senator's plan to create the Long Island Power Authority, a state-sanctioned utility that would take over the Long Island Lighting Company and, once and for all, kill off the dreaded Shoreham Nuclear Power Station, a controversial behemoth 15 miles north of my home town. After the meltdown at Three Mile Island and the jarring possibility of nuclear catastrophe from the movie, "The China Syndrome," the people were spooked over the reactor in their backyard, especially their inability to evacuate an island that's jammed up every rush hour. The utility's quest to put the plant on line sparked an epic war and it was my job as a reporter to cover the battles and now, as a senate aide, I was part of the effort to end it once and for all.

CHAPTER 36

MORE ABOUT HARVARD

The construction of the Shoreham plant was a boondoggle from day one and many Long Islanders benefitted from the billions that poured into this nuclear folly. What was once billed as a plant that could produce energy too cheap to meter became a bottomless money pit with the potential to irradiate the very people who had to pay for it.

We first felt the power of the nuclear plant when we played against Shoreham-Wading River, a school flush with tax money from the atomic installation. While we were a rag-tag bunch with hand-me-down uniforms stained from playing on dirt fields, the Shoreham players breathed from oxygen tanks on the sidelines and shined like they stepped out of a laundry commercial. We beat them anyway.

"Remember that game?" I reminisced with Harvard one night.

"How could I forget?"

We were playing for the league championship in soccer and the six-foot-four Harvard was our most violent attacker. The opponent's fullback was moving the ball and Harvard threw his body in for a perfectly executed sliding tackle, a move where as long as you touch the ball first, it's a clean play if the opponent trips over you and goes down. The referee didn't see it that way, of course, and ejected Harvard from the game. With the big lunk fuming on the sidelines, we went on to lose the title.

In the spring, we were slotted to play for the baseball championship on the day that happened to be senior cut out day.

If you cut, you couldn't play and the only kids left in the classrooms were ballplayers and nerds. Among the missing was Harvard, who decided it would be more fun to party than compete for the title. I was just back after missing 16 games from being spiked in the knee during a play at the plate and a black kid, Cliff, was happy to have me take back my job as catcher. The championship was an away game in Westhampton and we took a one run lead into the bottom of the last inning. With two men on and two outs, the batter smacked a sharp grounder to the pitcher who snatched it up with practically all day to throw it over to first. He probably could have walked the ball there himself. In fact, he could have gotten it there in time on his knees pushing it with his nose. Instead, he reared back and rocket-launched it over the first basemen's head, a shorter guy who was filling in for the missing Harvard. We stood there helpless as the tying run scored, then the winning run. Due to the fact that I broke my wrist skateboarding and didn't make the college team the following year, it was the last baseball game I ever played.

After college we assembled the best of the best to create a soccer team that was nearly invincible. Of the 11 starters, seven were black and four were white, all faces from the crowd at the shopping center riot years before. I was in the goal and Harvard was back at his familiar slot on the front line. We played together so instinctively we didn't need a coach and at the end of our first season in the Peconic League, the Center Moriches Attack took an undefeated record into the championship game. With time running out and the score deadlocked at zero, Harvard executed a perfect sliding tackle and freed up the ball for what would have been an easy score by our closing linemen. But it was déjà vu all over again as it dawned on us all at once that it was the same referee as the high school game way back when. Harvard was again booted from the game. This time, however, he wasn't going to take it lightly. While everyone was focused on the action on the field, Harvard came running out of the woods with a huge tree limb and started chasing the referee. The team brought him to the ground before he could do any damage and though Harvard's intensity inspired us to win the game, we were thrown out of the league. As team president, I appealed to the board of directors and they let us back in under the condition Harvard had nothing to do with the team.

The next season, another team in the Peconic League, which was made up of Spanish busboys and kitchen workers from the Coram Pond Diner, along with the Greeks who ran it, disagreed with a call and chased the ref off the field. They rocked his van trying to tip it over as he drove off and were banned from the league. The following week we were scheduled to play them at home and they showed up—so we played them. That got us kicked out once and for all.

It was a pisser playing soccer with such a diverse group and after the games we shared beers and laughs. We celebrated right on the field and after one championship I took pictures of the beaming athletes. They really let their hair down, and their shorts for that matter, as they mooned the camera. It was always tough getting clear pictures of our team because if you made the print too dark, you couldn't see the black guys. If you lightened it, you'd wash out the whities. I dropped off the roll at Photo Hut. A few days later I picked it up only to find that they mishandled the order and I got back prints from a very formal Italian wedding. I imagined the shock of that family gathered in the living room when they opened our pictures.

"Vive l'Tak!"

Before he left high school, Harvard was offered a full scholarship to play baseball at the University of Florida, a sure shot at playing in the pros for an athlete of his caliber. Harvard never had a chance to live that dream, however. His father said no, preferring him to work in the family construction business instead.

CHAPTER 37

THE FOUR BLACK MEN

John looked up from his chair at four imposing black men. They were the power brokers of Harlem and New York City and America and suddenly, the covers of George Magazine and all the trappings of his life that adorned the walls around him seemed so trivial.

Before him stood a man whose shirt was stained by the blood of Dr. Martin Luther King that fateful day on the balcony. There also stood a national civil rights leader and a mayor and a man who had been an associate of Malcolm X.

"Moynihan's out," the first one said, the words sending John's mind spinning like the moments of your life before you die. Moynihan was New York's senator for a quarter century. His job, and all of the men in the room knew it, would be John's stepping stone to the world's highest office—president of the United States.

"We ask that you be our next senator."

The magazine editor knew this moment would come, yet it still struck him like a blow to the gut. John could have entered the world of politics anytime he wanted, especially after his stellar performance at the Democratic National Convention. But he wanted to wait. He wanted to make something of himself outside of politics. He wanted to make his mark in business and George was his vehicle. He wanted real world experience, trials and tribulations and lessons learned that he could take into government. He didn't want to be a politician for the sake of politics. He wanted to be a man of the world and a leader and he wanted a solid foundation to stand on just like his father, the war hero. He wanted to be able to make a difference.

He looked up at the Four Men, all of whom declined his offer to be seated.

"What about Hillary?" was all he could muster.

"Don't worry about her," another of the men said of the former first lady. "Maybe secretary of state."

It was clear their thoughts were well beyond the senate. They were there to recruit a president.

Carolyn was delighted. From the day they met, there's no denying it, she harbored the dream. To all the catty girls in college, the echelons of Manhattan and the embarrassing list of Hollywood A-listers and models John bedded before her, she would trump them all. First Lady!

The aspiring young man pictured the conversation he would have had with his mother had she been alive to see the day.

"No. No way. Over my dead body," Jacqueline Kennedy Onassis said, glaring at her son with tears welling in her eyes.

"Mom, I don't think I can stop this," he replied to the twice-widowed matriarch whose grief in history made her more than just his mother. "I can't help but believe this is how it was meant to be."

Jackie gathered her thoughts. She must have known the day would come and just saying no would not be enough. After John's father was killed, Jackie moved the family to New York to give them an inkling of anonymity, and then married one of the richest men in the world, 23 years her senior, so John would have a father figure worthy of a president.

"The world kills Kennedys," she finally said, "and I don't think you should make yourself anymore of a target than you already are."

"I would be protected, mother. I can protect myself," he would have assured her.

"Dear Lord, John, you have a beautiful wife and a great life, why would you ever want to put us through this again?"

"I'm sorry, mother. It's my destiny."

John's entrance into the senate race sent shockwaves through the Clinton Camp.

Son of a bitch! the former president thought to himself as the former first lady pondered her new odds. The dynamic duo had their own sense of history and America's first women president was on Hillary's mind practically from the day they got to Washington. Sure, there were bumps along the way, not the least of which was Bill's dalliances, including his Oval Office fling with Monica Lewinsky that led to his impeachment. Yet, Hillary stood by her man. She suffered ridicule and derision from an exasperated public, but she held her head high. She earned—no, she deserved—the presidency.

In the days to follow, John's schedule spun out of control as it was taken over by the Four Men. They paraded him before brokers and bankers, politicians and players. They all offered money, and plenty of it. Everyone wanted to be in on the ground floor. With New York one of the nation's most reliable Blue States with Democrats outnumbering Republicans four to one, and as the son of the nation's most revered Democrat and a huge celebrity in his own right, John F. Kennedy, Jr. was a shoo-in to replace Moynihan. He went before the editors of the New York Times and the leaders of Congress. He dined with ambassadors and went to galas with millionaires and billionaires. He thought they saw him as the Second Coming of Christ. At home, late one exhausting night, he said to Carolyn: "I wonder when I get to meet the voters."

CHAPTER 38

THE ENEMA *WAS* NEEDED

My life took an entirely different course from that of the vaunted Scion of Camelot. Eight months into my stint with Senator LaValle, I got a call from a former Suffolk Life colleague, Pete Scully, who had left for greener pastures to become a legislative aide to the Brookhaven Town Board. He was the one who got a $15 prize from Readers Digest for penning the line: "The explosion was attributed to a buildup of gas by town officials."

One time when I took a bathroom break, Scully changed a quote in a story I was working on to say that according to the town supervisor…"the enema was needed." The editor didn't think it was too funny, but considering that particular politician, would probably have agreed the enema was, in fact, needed.

In the political world, good reporters were hot commodities because we covered everything. We went to the town board meetings, planning boards, zoning boards, civic meetings, all sorts of hearings, and we didn't just sit there, we interviewed the key players and wrote stories that were read by many. We knew more about what was going on than the politicians. For people whose livelihoods depended on getting elected, having guys like us on the staff was a big plus.

It was fun reminiscing with Scully about our time at the paper. The newsroom was small and our chairs practically touched as we banged out the week's news on dilapidated typewriters. If you made a mistake, you used scissors to cut out the bad part and taped in the correct version. I'm probably one of a few writers who started out on a manual Olivetti typewriter in college and switched to electric and then to computers when Suffolk Life moved to its new, state-of-the-art headquarters.

When I was on the phone once interviewing a guy named Dick Blowes, Scully laughed so hard in the background I could hardly talk. Then there was the bar owner on Dune Road whose customers kept crossing over private property to get to the beach. The homeowners filed a lawsuit accusing the patrons of "fornicating, defecating, and urinating" on their land. When I called for a comment, he steadfastly denied anyone was "fucking, shitting, or pissing anywhere."

The all-time classic was the photo of the big white duck that appeared on the paper's front cover. A farmer built the 20-foot tall roadside icon in 1931 to advertise his poultry business and with its two automobile tail lights for eyes, grew into a popular tourist attraction. The caption was supposed to read, "The Big White Duck, a giant symbol of the famous Long Island delicacy," but someone made a typo and a new delicacy, The Big White Dick, debuted in 250,000 editions.

Along with writing stories, we were responsible for taking pictures and the pressure was on every week to come up with a shot for the front cover. One deadline morning, the editor himself, Lou Grasso, came in with a roll he said had a great shot of a horse basking in a field. The only problem was the Angel that worked in the darkroom called in sick and he sent me in to develop his precious film. Lou was craggy and brusque and called everyone "Bubala." Seeing how I never developed film before and was shown only once how to do it by the Darkroom Angel, I was scared shitless going into the tiny little room.

The process starts with taking the film out of its tin case and wrapping it onto a special reel. In the dim red light of the darkroom this seemed a lot easier when the Angel did it. I was sweating bullets, almost puking from the chemical smells. Next, you have to mix a batch of the developer and take the temperature of the resulting formula. A stained chart on the wall told you how many minutes to soak the film for your particular temperature, but first

I needed to know what type of film Lou used, so it was into the garbage to find the tin I had thrown away.

The film then goes into a canister with a handle on the top so you can continuously mix the batch by spinning the reel. Or you could simply shake it up and down like the Darkroom Angel did when she came out for fresh air. I had a crush on her and always looked forward to her coming out of her cave. I, on the other hand, didn't dare set foot into the light of day and spun the mixture like a mad scientist with my eyes glued to the clock.

After your specific time, the development process has to be stopped by taking the film out and plunging it into a rinse. At this point, if you are brave, you could give it a peak to see how it turned out. Not me, and I let the film soak for a good 10 minutes before looking.

"What's going on in there," Grasso pounded on the door, not daring to come in and ruin the process. "We have a paper to put out."

"Almost done," I answered meekly.

With a deep breath and the editor's wrath looming, I checked the film. It came out okay. With the weight of the world off my shoulders, I figured I'd have a little fun. During one of my frantic Monday morning drives searching for a cover shot, I took a few pictures of a concrete donkey statue someone thought would be nice to display on their front lawn. With Lou's negatives on the drying rack, I put my film in the enlarger and burned off a couple of prints of the blanched burro. This process is less nerve wracking than developing film because if you screw up, you can always try again.

The enlarger is simply a projector that shoots your image onto photographic paper for a few seconds or so. Then it's into another chemical bath where you can see the image take shape before your eyes. If it's too light, get another sheet and expose it longer. Too dark, less time. When the picture looks okay, fish it out of the bath, rinse it, and pop it into the dryer. I squashed down my pile of rejects in the garbage to hide them.

When I got the editor's pictures right I bounded out of the darkroom gasping like I just brought Frankenstein to life.

"I think they came out a little funny," I said, handing the prints to Lou.

His face flushed a full suite of emotions from horror to humor to anger as he realized the pale mule wasn't his scenic horse.

"You better have the right ones, Bubala."

I wondered if John's mom, Jackie Bouvier, had this much fun when she was an Inquiring Photographer for The Washington Times-Herald.

CHAPTER 39

DEARIE

One time, for want of a quicker trigger finger, I missed a photo that surely would have won me a Pulitzer Prize. I was covering a hearing on whether Suffolk County should accept a federal grant to fund abortion counseling. The clerk called the name of the first speaker and the large doors of the legislative auditorium swung open. Approaching the microphone was a frail but plump young girl escorted at each elbow by two rather stern looking gentlemen.

"I am carrying my father's child," she told the legislators, the upshot being that abortion counseling, particularly in her case, would be a good thing. Everyone's jaw dropped except for Legislator Rose Caracappa, a staunch pro-life Conservative, who sat there stone-faced and seething at the set up.

Next at the microphone was Bill Baird, the acknowledged father of reproductive rights. Jailed eight times in five states for lecturing on birth control and abortion, Baird was behind three Supreme Court victories, including Eisenstadt vs. Baird, a landmark case that allows unmarried persons to possess contraception. He told the crowd he began his crusade after witnessing an unwed mother of nine bleed to death after a coat hanger abortion she performed on herself. Baird travelled the nation distributing contraceptives from his "Plan Van" and when he wasn't locked up, dodged firebombs from pro-life extremists. He was one of the first to drill clinic workers in counter-terrorism measures.

Legislator Caracappa would have none of it and challenged Baird at every turn. As she ripped him for his career as a "baby killer," Baird muttered, "Perhaps we should take a look into your background, dearie."

"I'll see you outside," the legislator countered and stormed out the door behind the dais. Baird went out the front.

A regular at the auditorium, I knew it would take a moment for Caracappa to wend her way to the lobby where Baird was waiting. I envisioned a photo of the two with fingers in each other's twisted faces, mouths agape, arguing and positioned myself to get the money shot. The legislator's clopping heels ricocheted through the corridor as she approached and instead of the animated discourse I imagined, she screamed, "You son of a bitch," and swung a haymaker at Baird's head that would have made Muhammad Ali proud.

It takes a 60th of a second to snap a picture, but it took Caracappa less than that to take her swing. The only picture I got was of her storming off.

For the record, Caracappa missed. If she had connected, she would have broken every bone in her hand, not to mention Baird's face. That's what I told the myriad of lawyers, anyway, since each side sued the other for zillions. For ever after, I live with the photograph I didn't get of the Conservative's fist whizzing by the abortion guy's nose, one with a look of sheer insult and the other bug-eyed in disbelief.

It wasn't the first time I was grilled by competing attorneys. The very weekend before I was to start my job as a reporter with Suffolk Life I was woken by a commotion from across the street. The cops had pulled over a trio of local boys and proceeded to beat the crap out of them with billy clubs when they resisted arrest. I memorialized the event with my new camera, a college graduation gift from the family. One of the cops tried to confiscate it. I told him I was with Suffolk Life Newspapers and he did not have the right, so he left me alone.

I knew there would be a problem with the pictures. Since the flash was on back order, the late night shots came out blurry and so, with no clear, corroborating evidence, I couldn't bolster the case of either side and they left me out if it.

CHAPTER 40

SHADMORE

Working at Suffolk Life gave me a sideshow seat to a tragic and tawdry episode played out under the harsh lights of Broadway. I received a call from a man named Norman Kean who was upset over a development project on the bluffs of Montauk overlooking the Atlantic Ocean near his summer home. The land is of magnificent beauty with a panoramic view of eastern Long Island and towering dunes cascading down to the sea. Montaukett Indians lived there for eons and it once served as Camp Wycoff where Teddy Roosevelt and his Rough Riders were quarantined for malaria after their exploits in the Spanish-American War. During World War Two it was used as a coastal artillery station and concrete bunkers that housed 16-inch guns remain there today. Now it's known as Shadmore, after the heathland shadbush that grows there.

"They're salting the wells," Kean told me, rather emphatically. "They can't build there because there's not enough fresh water and they're faking the test results. They're salting the wells, I say, and it's wrong."

I wrote a story about Shadmore and Mr. Kean's opposition to the 100-acre development plan. The attention focused concern on the fragile island's ability to provide water for such a large development and the approval process ground to a halt. Norman Kean was delighted.

Soon after, a letter came to the office inviting me to attend the Tenth Anniversary of the musical, Oh! Calcutta!, and backstage passes to the cast party. It turns out that Norman Kean was not only the producer of the play which was, at the time, the longest-running revue on Broadway, but also owned the Edison Theater where it was staged.

I went with my newspaper colleagues and Mr. Kean could not have been a better host. The seats were great and I took further advantage of his hospitality by scoring front row tickets to the show a few weeks later for me and a few friends.

Oh! Calcutta! was not your typical Broadway fare. The performers do their thing entirely in the nude and in the 1980's it was a sensation as people came from all over the world to see young ladies and men sing and dance in the buff. In fact, its title is taken from a painting by Clovis Trouille, itself a pun on "O quel cul t'as," French for "What an arse you have!" One of its sketches was penned by none other than John Lennon.

It was an interesting experience to go backstage as a friend of Mr. Kean's and party with actors who moments before were traipsing around in their birthday suits.

As for Shadmore, New York State took over the place and made it a nature preserve, one of the premier expanses of open space on the Eastern Seaboard. Too bad Norman Kean didn't live to see the day. He had discovered his wife of many years, an actress with the peculiar name of Gwyda DonHowe, was having an affair and after their 14-year old son headed off to school one morning, stabbed her to death. When the maid arrived, he gave her some letters, one of which stated that the show, Oh! Calcutta!, must go on, and plunged himself from his 18th story apartment to the courtyard below.

CHAPTER 41

ADULATION

Hillary and Bill Clinton said to each other, "What the hell," and decided to challenge John Kennedy for the U.S. Senate. The Four Men felt spurned by the Clintons since they made it clear that the senate was John's stepping stone to the White House and he would make Hillary secretary of state. The former president and first lady scoffed at the idea and the Four Men doubled down on their favored son. John would announce his candidacy in their wheelhouse, a coronation at the famed Apollo Theater in Harlem.

On the big day, something seemed extraordinary to the engineer on the #2 Train to West 125th Street. The conductors and riders on the other lines couldn't help but notice it too. And so did the cabbies and bus drivers across the city and the toll takers at the crossings. People were streaming into Manhattan like lemmings and making their way to Harlem where John F. Kennedy, Jr. was to appear in the flesh.

There were laborers, nurses and clerks, students playing hooky and retirees, some of whom had crashed the tarmac at John F. Kennedy Airport in 1964 to greet the Beatles. People from the projects, the suburbs, Long Island and upstate flowed in a sea of humanity toward West 125th Street, known also as Dr. Martin Luther King, Jr. Boulevard, to be part of history.

John had arrived at the Apollo earlier and huddled in a dressing room with the Four Men. They had distributed tickets to their political friends and the theater was packed. The SRO crowd jostled with reporters and dozens of photographers clogged the aisles.

John peeked out from behind a side curtain and swallowed hard. He was more uneasy than backstage the time he went on Oprah. He was, he felt, more nervous than he's ever been in his life. He had a secret, though, to help him cope, something he knew his father did and it worked every time. He closed his eyes and took in a deep breath and focused on nothing but that breath and he felt the tension start to drain. There were no thoughts in his mind except the pure energy of the air that flowed in and out of his lungs. There was no crowd, no pressure, no senate, no presidency, just himself in his mind as calm as he could be.

It was a different story outside the Apollo Theater. West 125th Street was jammed with people, cabs and cars from Adam Clayton Powell, Jr. Boulevard all the way to Frederick Douglas. Traffic ground to a halt and police cordoned off the area at Lenox Avenue to the east and west to Morningside, three blocks over.

Reporting from a helicopter overhead, WABC News reporter Ian Andrews estimated the crowd at over a quarter million.

"Fans of John F. Kennedy, Jr. have shut down Harlem's major thoroughfares in what looks to be a vain attempt to glimpse the man who may very well be our next senator from New York and, if the sea of support here in upper Manhattan is any indication, the next president of the United States," Andrews reported.

The Four Men worried that a riot would break out and each calculated in their mind the impact trampled bodies, looting and chaos would have on their man's future.

John witnessed the scene on a television in his dressing room. The crowds were contained for now, but even in his seclusion he could sense the volatility. They had come to see him and had no chance of even getting close.

A New York City police detective filled them in: "We've called in reinforcements—MTA cops, National Guard, other jurisdictions. It's going to take a while, but we think we can handle them."

"No," John interrupted, "I have to go on now."

"You can't. We need time to get the situation under control."

"Right now," and he headed for the door. The largest of the Four Men blocked it.

"Tell him he has to wait," the detective ordered.

The black man was taller than John and beefier. He was older and stared at him with a countenance honed from years of confrontation and dispute. John glared back and the two men engaged in a fierce battle with their eyes. To everyone in the room, John was no longer a tousle-headed boy gliding through the world. He projected a force shaped by tragedy, determination, and a deep sense of destiny. A tremendous might radiated from his steely eyes. The big man wilted.

"He's the boss," the sentry relented and stepped aside. The detective careened after him but the big man blocked his path.

"It's time."

The crowd erupted as John's first foot hit the stage and those in the know girded for an ovation sure to last a minute or longer.

John strode to the microphone and yelled, "I want everyone to be quiet right now."

Most of the people couldn't hear and the roar of their adulation continued.

"Everyone, please. Quiet. Now!" he yelled again.

The room fell silent like someone hit the mute button.

"I want everyone to listen carefully. The people outside this theater, everyone who can hear me, turn up your radios. The people of Harlem, you shop owners, people in your cars, cab drivers, turn up your radios. Turn them up loud so everyone can hear."

John knew he was carried live and every station in the city was broadcasting his every word.

"Everyone! Everyone who can hear my voice, please share my words. Share them with your neighbors. Share them with the people in the streets. I speak with one voice, your voice, and I want everybody to hear it."

Drivers stuck in traffic rolled down their windows and cranked up the volume. Kids appeared with boom boxes and residents pointed their radios toward the street.

John held his fingers to his lips, the Apollo audience was at his command. He held his hand over the microphone and said to a crowd so quiet you could hear their hearts beat: "Okay. Everyone hush. I'm going to see if the people outside can hear me."

He yelled into the mic: "The people of Harlem. The people of New York City, our great state of New York and the United States of America, can You Hear Me?"

The audience in the Apollo Theater didn't just hear the response, they felt it. East from the Harlem River and west from the Hudson, the people roared so loud they vibrated the walls of the theater.

"I know. I know," he repeated until the crowd died down, "I know you can't be inside of the Apollo Theater with me today. There just isn't enough room for everyone. But that's okay. You can hear me and I can hear you."

Another roar shook the rafters and this time John let the ovation continue for a good two minutes. The people in the streets were ecstatic. They did not have to see him to know he was with them. John meant his words for each one of them and everyone who made the pilgrimage to Harlem and everyone who listened on the radio and saw history unfold on TV, felt he was speaking to them personally.

"Thank you," he said, his words bringing a fresh round of acclaim.

"Thank you. Thank you very much."

The crowds, both inside and out, roared louder.

"Thank you. Thank you so very much."

Every time he spoke the people erupted and each time, he had to step back and let them go.

He approached the mic again and this time commanded, "Okay, everyone quiet please," causing silence to fall across Manhattan.

"I take this stage not as John F. Kennedy, Jr. or the son of a president, but as a voice," he said without the benefit of notes. "I come before you as your voice, as the voice of the people, and you have my promise that wherever I go, whatever I do, I will speak not for myself, but for you."

The crowds again went wild and in the wings, the Four Men beamed. Carolyn watched the event on TV from her office and held her scarf to her eyes. She could feel the elation of everyone around her.

"I am here today to announce my candidacy for the United States Senate to try and fill the shoes of the magnificent Daniel Patrick Moynihan, a man I could only hope to emulate."

The crowds wouldn't let him get too far and interrupted again with cheers. His words came in short bursts.

"From now to Election Day I will work tirelessly to earn your support."

Rabid applause.

"I will take your concerns to Washington and make our state a better place."

Another ovation.

"You will see a lot of me in the coming days and I will be at your side here in the streets of Harlem and the cities and villages of our great state and I will be your voice in the nation's Capitol. Thank you. Thank you for your support and I look forward to seeing you again soon."

Pandemonium.

John strode off the stage, his hand waiving to the adoration. Backstage he asked one of the Four Men to do him a favor. "I want you to go into the streets and bring in some people, some average people who live here."

"Ok, boss."

"Not the people from the audience, but the people from the neighborhood. Maybe a dozen or so. I want to hear from them."

On the other side of town, the Clinton's were dumbfounded. It was a spectacle Bill had hardly seen as president and they both knew it would be an impossible to beat the Boy Prince.

"What do you think, honey?"

"I think secretary of state sounds pretty good."

John penned a message for George Magazine:

My Dear Readers:

George strives to bring you the latest in politics as it converges with our lives. Whether it's violence in the movies or free speech on the Internet, gay marriage, war—a never-ending cavalcade of issues—our culture drives politics and George has been at the forefront to illuminate the impact.

That said, I've been presented with a unique opportunity, a chance to serve as senator of the United States. I've always wanted to do something outside of politics—serve as a prosecutor, be a success in the business world, learn the issues and concerns of the everyday man and woman and then bring that real-life experience into government. While this learning process probably will never end, and I would have wanted to stay at the helm of George for much longer, the wheels of fate will not wait and I'm presented with a stunning opportunity to take the next step in my life.

While I could never hope to fill the extraordinary shoes of the great Daniel Patrick Moynihan, I will give it my best and hope, with my dear readers at my side, I can be a worthy senator.

There are some who believe this is a stepping stone to an ultimate goal—president of the United States. But let's take it one step at a time. As senator, I will focus on the needs of my home state, New York, and the needs of my country. Ours is a great nation, though it's not necessarily great for everyone. Some people, through no fault of their own, find the deck stacked against them; that the land of opportunity leaves no opportunity for them. What would we be if we didn't lift everyone up to become greater so we can all live prosperous and free?

Fortunately, I'm leaving George in the great hands of a capable staff who will continue to see the political world through imaginative eyes and deliver the content that makes our magazine interesting and great. You will hear from me often and I hope I can live and learn and serve this nation with you, together.

Yours Always,
John

CHAPTER 42

ONE TAKE TOMMY

Back in my mundane life, my old newspaper friend Pete Scully was being promoted to deputy town supervisor and wanted to know if I was interested in taking his old job as legislative aide. It came with a $7,000 raise over what I was making in the state senate and, more appealing, my own town vehicle. I jumped at the chance, but was tormented by the thought of breaking it to Senator LaValle who appreciated my work and had just given me a small bonus. He tried to talk me out of going to Brookhaven, warning me it was a political swamp and not a great place to work. I went anyway and he gracefully turned down my offer to give back the bonus.

Seeing how I had my own office and a car to take home, working at town hall seemed like a big step up. My job was to create an image of the town board members who, if the public really knew what they did all day, would never get voted back in. One used to walk around with an armful of files containing the development applications, zone changes, variances and other favors town officials could bestow on their friends to make them rich. The councilman gave no illusions that his job was to actually serve the public and we had all we could do to create some kind of persona that would keep him from being kicked out. In government, the incumbents almost always win, unless they're caught doing something unseemly in Macy's window. One of the reasons why is they can spend taxpayer dollars to hire people like me to promote them. Grudgingly, they had to show up to a studio once in a while to record "public service" announcements to enlighten the masses. One such session went like this:

"This is town councilman uhh..."

"Cut."

"This is umm, town councilman..."

"Cut."

"Reminding everybody to ahh, duh..."

"Cut."

This went on for a good 20 minutes until the tongue-tied councilman threatened to quit. Surely running though a few sentences without any uhhs and duhs was possible and we convinced him to try some more. After flubbing line after line, he was able to do the last sentence without a mistake and the sound engineer, who finally had enough, called it quits saying he could piece the words together to make something reasonable. On the way out I remarked, "That was great! You did it in one take," meaning the last line. "That's right," the councilman replied, "I'm One Take Tommy."

Back at town hall, he told everybody how well the recording went and it wasn't long until he sparked the interest of a reporter. The inquiry morphed into a tale of One Take Tommy waltzing into the studio, nailing the commercial in one shot, and leaving to the amazed adoration of the staff. To those who knew him this was amazing indeed.

Chapter 43

THE OMEN

"Two gentlemen to see you, John. They don't have an appointment," the receptionist's voice informed the busy senator.

"I don't have time. Find out what they want and we'll get back to them."

"It's a very old man, says his name is Gasa. And the other...I think you should come out here."

John was greeted by a sturdy black man, about his age, and was startled by how familiar he looked. The other man was also black, very black, his head shriveled from the sun. John stood there stunned. He knew exactly who they were.

"Mr. Kennedy!" the older man exclaimed, falling into him. John grasped his arms and held him upright. The man fought his tears.

"My name is Biuku Gasa. I was a friend of your father's. And this, this is somebody I want you to meet. This is my John, John F. Kennedy. We named him after the president."

The younger man beamed, his perfect white teeth shining like a lamp.

"Please, please come in," John finally said. "Can we get you something, something to drink?

The pair nodded no and followed the publisher into his office.

"I want to thank you for saving my father's life and his crew," John spoke up. "The coconut, we kept it all these years. It's in the Presidential Library in Boston. I can take you there to see it if you want."

Gasa looked at him with dead serious eyes.

"You can't do it, Mr. Kennedy. "Please don't do it."

"Do what?"

"Run for president. It's not safe for you. Please don't be the president."

John knew that Biuku Gasa and the other islander, Eroni Kumana, came to America to reunite with his father and were turned around after the assassination. This was his first time back in the states.

"I appreciate it. I appreciate you coming here so much," John got the words out, not knowing what to say next.

"We saved your father," Gasa said, "and he went on to great things and then he died. It was a tragedy, so much of an impact on our lives and we cannot hardly live with it even now. A great man and then no more."

Gasa kept his eyes locked on John's making him powerless to look away.

"It cannot happen to you, John Kennedy. Please, live your life free and safe. Don't be the president."

John looked away to Gasa's son. The man's expression had turned severe as if he was willing John to change the course of history. "If something were to happen to you, we would be ruined," he told the scion.

"I appreciate your thoughts and well wishes, I really do. But it's different now. The president is well protected. Nothing like that would ever happen again."

Gasa cut him off. "Fate can be changed. We have seen that, we know it can be done. Your life gives you choices, but you don't have to take them. You can control your destiny."

John was devastated by the words.

"If you choose not to be president, you will live a long time. If you choose that path, it will be different."

"But I'm running for senator, not president."

"We know what the senate means. Please, Mr. Kennedy, please don't do it."

CHAPTER 44

THE VOICE OF THE PEOPLE

It was John himself who found the solution to the crowd problem. He couldn't go to a civic meeting or a Democratic club to campaign like a normal candidate, else he would be mobbed, so he was forced to meet the people en masse.

"Stadiums. I want us to book the largest stadiums in every major city in New York State," he told his staff. "If people have the desire to come see me, I want to make it easy for them."

For his campaign manager, John's run for the senate turned politicking upside down.

"It's not a normal race," the manager told the staff. "We don't need TV commercials or mailings, heck, we don't even need fundraisers. We just have to let people know where he's going to be and let nature do the rest."

From Buffalo's Ralph Wilson Stadium and the Carrier Dome in Syracuse to Shea Stadium in Queens and the Nassau Coliseum on Long Island, John appeared before the people. He even left the state and packed Giants Stadium in New Jersey.

His message was the same: "I hear the voice of all the people and will become your voice if you elect me as your man in Washington."

Some reporters picked up on the fact that nobody seemed to care about the issues, but it didn't matter. When it came to John Kennedy, not much was mentioned about taxes or war or Social Security or any issues of the day. Running for the senate seemed a mere formality for the man who would be president and the people just wanted to see him and be a witness to history.

The biggest event on the tour by far was at Yankee Stadium which drew people from not only New York and surrounding states, but across the U.S. and throughout the world. That's when Hillary Clinton appeared on the stage and endorsed the Prince. He was gracious and humble and she was effervescent with a plastic smile that seemed to be painted on her face. Bill grumbled in the background and across town, in a small Manhattan suite, John's challenger on the Republican ticket, Congressman Rick Lazio, rued his decision to give up his safe house seat to take on the most popular man on the planet. During their one public appearance together, in a televised debate at a mutually-agreed upon secret location, Lazio strode across the stage and demanded that John sign a document he called a "New York Freedom From Soft Money Pledge." John waived him off and Lazio skulked away as a mere footnote in the history of politics.

John's electrifying success gave the Four Men a new, unexpected role: making deals with Republicans who didn't want John to campaign against them. Though New York was a solid Democrat state, there were pockets of GOP dominance and the last thing the politicians in those areas needed was John siding with their opponents. He told the Four Men early on that he wasn't going to upset anyone's apple cart, despite repeated requests from the party bosses, but that didn't stop the Four Men. They liked to see the elephants squirm and took great satisfaction in lording John over those who questioned their power.

"Make me one promise," Carolyn told John the day he decided to run. "Do not ever fly your plane to Washington, or anywhere else for that matter, without an instructor sitting next to you."

The implications were clear to John and he was sure that night off Martha's Vineyard was always fresh in his wife's mind.

"But honey, I'm so close to finishing my instrument certification," he protested.

"Do you want me to tell the world you're not fit to be senator?"

Boy, the woman really knows how to play hardball, John thought to himself.

"Okay, okay. It's a promise. No flying without an instructor. But what about after I'm certified."

"You get the certificate and then we'll talk."

John couldn't protest too much because Carolyn was such a trooper on the campaign trail and didn't break his chops over all of the time they spent apart. Plus, flying safe was in his own best interest. He blanched to think of the grief and sorrow his crashing that night would have wrought. While Carolyn should have fretted over John's rapid political ascension given the Kennedy family history, she was okay with it and privately relished the thought of a Washington life.

John's election to the U.S. Senate was a foregone conclusion and he spent the last few weeks of the campaign turning over the duties at George with the promise that he would drop in regularly and write a column from time to time. He beat Congressman Lazio with a record 89 percent of the vote.

CHAPTER 45

WHY DO YOU ASK?

In stark contrast to the supernova career of John Kennedy, my life was filled with more mundane chores such as going to meetings of the Brookhaven Town Board. They met in a cramped room in the basement of town hall and this brought together, elbow to elbow, secretaries, staffers, reporters, and anyone else compelled to attend their so-called "work" sessions.

One morning while the crowd was shoe-horning itself in and the room was still buzzing, Councilman Don Zimmer decided to tell me a joke. Of the six councilmembers, Zimmer was my favorite. Unlike many of the scheming weasels who float to the top of the political swamp, the former cash register salesman was always friendly and would do anything we suggested to promote his own self-interest. He did have one fault that would eventually kill him: Zimmer was a heavy smoker—cigarettes, cigars, pipes—lighting one off the other. He always smelled like he had been sitting by a bon fire and his fingers were stained a yellowish brown. His laughs were punctuated with a hacking wheeze.

One day Zimmer asked me to sit in on a meeting with a lady from Bellport, not far from the councilman's home town. She kept horses and was upset because they were all sick with cancer. She suspected the water which she said was polluted from a huge pit nearby that was used for years as a sump by a commercial laundry. Zimmer was well liked because he would actually meet with his constituents and had a salesman's face that expressed concern. "I love the people, and the people love me," he would tell us. He promised the lady he would have her water tested and she left satisfied that her councilman cared.

The test results were off the charts: heavy metals, pesticides, a whole smorgasbord of pollutants that could kill a horse, much less give it cancer. The town's public relations squad swung into action and we scheduled a press conference at the site. Leading the brigade was the board's new legislative aide, a freshly minted political science grad we called The Hack, or Hacka for short. Speculation was the Village of Bellport used the old laundry pit as a dump, but since we had no evidence of that, Zimmer was only to announce the results of the water tests and call on the state to investigate.

On the way over, Hacka briefed the councilman: "For legal reasons, Mr. Zimmer, make sure you don't mention the Village of Bellport."

"Call me Don," was his reply.

Knowing Zimmer a little better, I was a bit more emphatic: "Don't say anything about the Village of Bellport," Donald. "Don't even look in that direction. In fact, don't even use the words bell and port in the same sentence," I warned him.

The press conference was well attended by the media, in addition to the grateful neighbor and two lawyers from Bellport to make sure the town didn't impugn the esteemed village. With cameras rolling and the village's legal contingent holding up tape recorders, Zimmer got off to a great start: "Thank you everyone for being here today. I really appreciate it."

And then he panicked: "The water around here is all polluted. Just look at these test results…and it's all the Village of Bellport's fault."

The reporters scribbled frantically and the attorneys glanced down at their recorders to make sure the little wheels were still turning. Hacka almost had a heart attack.

We repaired to a local diner where we stared at Zimmer in disbelief. He ordered a bowl of pea soup and when Hacka grilled him on why he dragged Bellport into it, he went into a coughing fit that ended with him removing a chunk of green pork fat from his mouth and plopping it on the side of his plate. We thought he coughed up a piece of his lung, his just reward for blowing the press conference. The next day, he threw Hacka under the bus saying he was only repeating what the aide told him.

Despite our better judgment, we cooked up another "environmental" escapade and again put Zimmer and The Hack into the middle of it. Just south of the Shoreham nuclear plant is the Brookhaven National Laboratory, a research facility that helped usher in the Atomic Age after World War II. As part of the lab's safety protocols, they flew a surveillance mission over Long Island with special equipment and lo and behold, detected unnatural levels of radiation along somebody's hedgerow. This was at a time when an unprecedented building boom was engulfing Brookhaven and the town board was making favored land owners and developers millionaires practically overnight. Of course, people living next to paved-over farm fields and previously bucolic open spaces weren't so thrilled, so it was important to show that the town leaders were concerned about the environment.

We got a hold of a Geiger counter and unleashed Zimmer and Hacka on the scene. Leading a gaggle of very skeptical reporters around the property, Hacka couldn't get a reading so he cranked up the gadget's sensitivity. At this point, the background radiation from a cinderblock would have set it off and when he got near the "hot" zone, the Geiger counter started to click wildly. The reporters practically bowled over the councilman trying to get away. It turns out the home had been owned by a cesspool truck driver and at the end of the day he would hose out the tank and drain it into the bushes. Apparently, he washed out some radioactive waste from a barium enema or some such procedure he had picked up along the way and radiated the landscape.

Regardless, Zimmer's environmental cred was solidified, but we weren't done yet. Around this time, the cops caught some moron pumping dry cleaning waste into a town drainage basin and we proclaimed it an "act of environmental terrorism." Now it was One Take Tommy's turn to be the poster boy for the Green Movement. We raised the fine for dumping in a recharge zone to $10,000 and made up special warning signs for every drainage pool in town. The lawyers thought we were nuts and the insiders chuckled knowing old One Take cared as much for drainage sumps as he did for Himalayan yaks.

In the bowels of town hall, Councilman Zimmer shared his joke quietly with me, but the second he started, the room fell silent and everyone focused on him. Nervously scanning the crowd, he was compelled to continue:

A little Indian boy goes to the chief and asks, "How do you name all the people of our tribe?"

The Chief replied, "Oh, it's quite easy. When a baby is born, I look at the first thing I see moving in wilderness, and name it just that."

"How so?" asks the Indian boy.

"Well," replied the Chief, "if I see a coyote running in a field, I name the baby Running Coyote. If I see a bull sit, I name the baby Sitting Bull."

"Oh, now I see," says the boy.

Then the Chief turns to him and says, "Why do you ask, Two Dogs Fucking?"

CHAPTER 46

HENNY

The councilman let off a sheepish laugh and half the group snickered along with him, some bellowing loudly at the crude tale. The other half was aghast.

"You're sick, Donald," said the town supervisor, a salty Navy veteran by the name of Henrietta Acampora. Famous for sayings such as "They're not going to put the turd on my plate" and "I'm not going to let them put my tit in the ringer," Henny ruled the town with an iron hand. (To this day I cringe over the image of having one's tit put in the ringer.)

The Supervisor was wildly popular and to keep her in the headlines, we came up with a press conference that drew coverage from every media outlet in the tri-state area. New York did not have the death penalty even though both houses of the legislature approved it year after year. The problem was a veto from the governor and the inability of the assembly to conjure up the extra votes needed for an override. This year it came down to one vote and the media focused on a single assembly member, Earlene Hooper, as the potential tie breaker. In Brookhaven, Henrietta's town, a man was killed by someone who was previously jailed for murder, but was let out after a lengthy stay. We took Henny to meet the family of the dead man on the front steps of the county jail. Cameras rolling, she flawlessly delivered the line we prepared: "If we had the death penalty here in New York, we wouldn't be here with this family grieving over another senseless murder."

Assemblywoman Hooper would not be swayed and it was a number of years later when New York elected a Republican governor that the death penalty would finally be approved.

Game for pretty much anything Republican-Conservative, Henny was the headliner in one of the hardest-hitting political attacks the county had seen. A soap opera-looking politician named Pat Halpin had won the office of Suffolk County executive and was faced with the daunting task of drafting a budget that paid for all the promises he made to get elected. He was the first Democrat in years to win the seat and was such a darling of the liberal media that one paper actually did a story about his mustache. In contrast, his Republican opponent sported a rather unsightly birthmark across the better part of his cheek and was portrayed as an ogre in the side-by-side pics. We were in a meeting in Henny's office when the town comptroller came in shaking his head. "Halpin's budget has a 38 percent tax increase in Brookhaven," he told us, "and it's even worse in the other towns."

"Let's get him," the Supervisor replied.

We prepared a poison letter from Henny denouncing "High Tax Halpin" and the devastating affect his outrageous tax hike will have on senior citizens and especially the children. She asked for money to help fight this tax menace and we enclosed a postage-paid return envelope and a card where people could check off donations of $10, $25, $100, $500, $1,000 or other. A week after the mail hit, I went to the post office and my heart sank: all that was in our box was a note from the postmaster reading, "See me."

At the counter the clerk said, "So, you're the one," and disappeared into the back. A few trips later, she left me with four mail crates packed with envelopes. It took us a full day to open them and we had a blast reading the comments encouraging Henny to kick Halpin's ass. There were five donations of $1,000 and many people sent cash. In the end, we took in $17,000, enough to send out another mailing, this time with a caricature of High Tax Halpin from the Three Village Herald stating, "Confucius say: 'Beware of Pretty Face—Can Mask Unpretty Falsehood,'" and a "Repeal the County Tax" bumper sticker. We mailed the second round into Halpin's home town and it was assumed that three years hence, he stood no chance of being reelected.

One of the most remarkable displays of human interaction I ever witnessed occurred with Henny one morning in the town board's basement room. Shoreham opponents started getting the upper hand when the emergency backup generators at the nuclear plant broke down (they were dubbed "Snap, Crackle, and Pop) and the utility conducted an evacuation drill that pretty much proved you can't get 1.5 million people safely off an island. In response, the company decided to stop paying its taxes. With millions on the line, Henny assembled a group of county officials to push them into suing for the delinquent money. It was a precarious situation since the bulk of the tax dollars, collected from ratepayers across Long Island, flowed into Brookhaven. When one of the legislators, Rizzo, took exception to Henny's plea, she regaled him with a rash of expletives, finishing with her opinion that he lacked the necessary man parts to make a tough decision. In a rant heard around the world, Rizzo yelled back, "Fuck you, fuck you, fuck you," each time slapping his arm to project his middle finger at the Supervisor's face.

"I guess we can't count on your support then," Henny responded cool as a cucumber to the beet-red pol.

I had the occasion to ask Rizzo about the outburst a few months later. He told me his arm was sore for a week from so forcefully flipping Henrietta the bird.

CHAPTER 47

SILLY SEASON

The Supervisor's reelections normally came off without a hitch, but there was one incident that left us baffled. Labor Day usually marks the beginning of "Silly Season" when political campaigns begin in earnest. Because she had the money, Henny's camp wanted to get a jump on things and we developed a series of radio and newspaper ads set to hit two weeks prior. A week into it, nothing had come out and the team was going to meet after work to find out why.

The day was dominated by a news story about a town commissioner denying a Democrat congressman an audience at a town senior citizen club. These clubs were our turf and no interloping politician was going to mine them for votes. A local cable news station covered the controversy and we repaired to the dungeons of town hall to view the tape. It was here that an odd duck named McDonald took over a small room for Brookhaven's audio/visual operation which, up to that point, entailed only the copying and storing of the town board's public service announcements such as One Take Tommy's gem.

Someone in McDonald's family knew someone and seeing how he was on the payroll with nothing much to do, we had him work on the campaign, in particular delivering Henny's ads to the various stations and newspapers. He had a couple of TVs and VCR decks wired together and we kept pushing buttons until something lit up. Appearing on the screen, instead of the commissioner's news clip, was the most lurid sex scene between two men that you never wanted to imagine.

"Hey, that's not me," the commissioner objected as we scrambled for the eject button. In disbelief, we looked up at the shelf of town videos and noticed that many had their titles scratched out. Plugging them in one after another, we were treated to incredibly graphic displays of gay pornography. An all-points bulletin went out for McDonald and when we finally tracked him down in a town vehicle he had "borrowed," we discovered all of Henny's campaign advertising, undelivered, in the trunk.

Working on election campaigns wasn't without its hazards. Henny's opponent owned a restaurant on the Patchogue River that had docking space for a dozen or so boats. We received an anonymous tip that he made improvements to the dock without permits and called a press conference at the site, the sign for his business serving as the backdrop.

"How could he possibly be the town supervisor when he flaunts the critical environmental laws designed to protect our precious natural resources?" I asked the assembled media.

The barb hurt, so he sued me for $30 million, not so much for the money, but to keep me quiet. It didn't work and he lost the election, his biggest gambit being a press release criticizing Henny for replacing her office toilet with an expensive silent-flushing model.

I ran into him during the holidays. "Dick, I can't come up with whole $30 million right now," I told him. "Would you take half and maybe I can owe you the rest?" He laughed and a few weeks after that, dropped the thing altogether.

The Supervisor did recognize my contributions to her reelection effort and made me her executive assistant. From there, I became director of the town's Public Information Office. A pair of reporters from Newsday decided to have a little fun with me:

"Bob Chartuk figures that in his three years as aide to the town council, he's churned out an average of five press releases a week, 260 a year," they wrote.

"That could get pretty boring. So Chartuk has come up with a bold new way—literally—to spice up the releases.

"One day, while playing around with the town computer, he discovered that he could use bold face type to accent the most important parts of the press releases—namely the names of his bosses, the council members.

"For example, from a July 5 press release on the town's attempts to secure land at Shirley Beach: The land, off Grandview Drive on either side of Shirley Beach, will be kept 'forever wild,' **according to Councilman Don Zimmer.**

"And, from the same release: '**According to Councilman Zimmer,** the Town will also be moving to acquire additional land from Suffolk County north of Shirley Beach.'"

"Chartuk says it has nothing to do with politics or an election— after all, he boldfaced **Supervisor Henrietta Acampora's** name, and she's not running. At least not till next year.

"'The bottom line is, we're just doing it as a matter of style. We feel it adds to the visual impact of our work,'" Chartuk said.

"Actually, he pointed out, this isn't the first style change town press releases have undergone. A few years ago, Chartuk began justifying both margins so the releases would look neater. And a few months ago, Chartuk began boldfacing *and* underlining the titles across the top of the releases.

"What's next?

Chartuk isn't sure, but figures he'll come up with something.

"'When you write as many press releases as I do you figure out ways to make them look better over time,'" Chartuk said.

CHAPTER 48

BEDTIME FOR BILLY

The Republicans ruled Brookhaven and the only political conflicts were those that erupted within our own party. As supervisor, Henrietta pretty much controlled the GOP, mostly because she raised a lot of money and nobody had the balls (her words) to screw with her. The titular (ouch still) head of the party was an innocuous fellow they called Wally and the smart money walked a fine line between the Supervisor and the Chairman. Many political operatives were on the town payroll and were thus indentured to Henny, while an undercurrent operated in the background waiting for the old battleax to retire. From this group arose the Heritage Republican Club and its blue collar president, a town highway department worker who was being groomed for a bright political future by Wally and the highway superintendent himself. Their protégé spoke in terms of "dees" and "dose" and connected well with the town's working class. They called him Mugsy.

Hailing from a more upper crust part of the town was the area's only elected Democrat, Icilio Bianchi, the state assemblyman who went by the name of Bill. The Republicans knew they couldn't unseat him and never bothered, so when they had to find someone to run against him, came up with Sal Prisco, the Supervisor's former hairdresser who was on the town payroll serving pretty much as Henny's chauffer. No one gave any thought to the race until an opportunity to take an extraordinary photograph presented itself. The state assembly was holding a hearing on electric rates and I was there in the front row with my ever-present camera. At the dais were three legislators, two staring out at the audience quite intensely while the third, Bill Bianchi, was fast asleep with his head in his hand. Making matters worse, in front of the snoozing lawmaker was a huge name plaque loudly displaying his name, "I. William Bianchi, Member of the Assembly."

Click.

The mailing we did for Sal was titled, "Bedtime for Billy," and featured the embarrassing pic.

"Assemblyman Bill Bianchi catches a few winks during a recent Assembly committee hearing in Riverhead," it read.

"Actually, Brookhaven taxpayers might be a lot better off if he'd spent more time sleeping over the past twelve years," we rubbed it in.

"Unfortunately, Bianchi stayed awake long enough to vote to raise our taxes by over $1 billion during his career."

Ouch!

"Isn't it about time that career came to an end?—Sal Prisco, Assembly"

On election night, Prisco was ecstatic as poll results showed him neck and neck. But it wasn't to be. Sal lost by a handful of votes, a former hairdresser almost beating a 12-year incumbent. "If only they had taken the race seriously," Sal lamented, "I'd be an assemblyman."

The next time Bedtime Billy was up for election, I threw my hat in the ring. If an oversized hairdresser with an ungainly mustache could come that close, Billy would be no match for a widely-published former newspaper reporter hot-shot legislative aide such as myself. While Henrietta Acampora was behind me, the party Chairman had other ideas and without even giving me the time of day, anointed Mugsy for the race. I squawked, but it did me no good, and after throwing a few barbs at each other in the press, I sought to bury the hatchet with Wally. "As long as you don't bury it in my back," he said, "we're okay."

CHAPTER 49

YOUNG BUCKS

In an upset, Mugsy beat the assemblyman and the world didn't hear much from him until tragedy struck: his two-year-old son was killed by a mail truck. The political world went into mourning and it was decided it would be best for Mugsy to be at home, instead of Albany, so they named him to a vacant seat on the town board. The following November he stood for election and I went over to Democrat headquarters for some snooping. I headed in through the front door betting the receptionist had no clue who I was and asked for any information she could give me on their candidates. As she went to collect some pamphlets I noticed a stack of fliers on a desk and grabbed one. Back outside, I realized I had my hands on the most scandalous piece of campaign literature of the era. Someone created a handout about Mugsy titled, "How I Use My Dead Son For Political Gain." Back at our headquarters, the crew was apoplectic with Mugsy raving around the room threatening to kill whoever did it.

After easily winning the town board race, Mugsy's rise was meteoric. He became chairman of the town Republican Party and soon after, head of the county GOP. Controlling who gets to run for public office, and having a say in who these people hire and how they spend the public's money, gave Mugsy enormous power. Naturally, Mugsy's rise put the Acampora acolytes in a precarious position: on the one hand they were beholden to the lady who signs the checks while on the other, the balance of power was shifting back to the town party and the ascending Mugsy. The response was the creation of what Chairman Wally called a "Rump Group," the Monarch Republican Club, a more upscale version of Mugsy's Heritage Club whose president was a charismatic up-and-coming businessman known as the Monarch. While Mugsy was a dark-haired, blue collar chain smoker from suburbia, the Monarch was a fair-haired schmoozer with roots going back to the Mayflower. Wally and Mugsy would have preferred that the Monarch fell off a cliff and died, but the highway superintendent had a long history with his family and was behind him for a seat that opened up in the county legislature. The race quickly became not a contest of Republican vs. Democrat, but a manhood challenge between the two young bucks. As the Republican leader, Mugsy did his best to hamper the effort such as giving the opposition a head start by not officially naming the Monarch as the candidate until the very last minute. It would have surprised no one if he had already made a deal with the other side. It was a Monarch race and the few Heritage Club members who came to the headquarters were there as spies hoping to score points with their leader by reporting back what they saw. We knew we couldn't count on any help from Mugsy's side of the house, but little did we know it would be Henny's branch that would drag the Monarch's into the loser's column.

CHAPTER 50

MCNAMARA'S BAND

A week before the vote, Monarch loyalist Joey Mac came into the campaign office agitated and pale. He was a salesman at McNamara Buick-Pontiac and reported that the feds were raiding the dealership. They created a traffic jam on Nesconset Highway by carting off every car and truck from McNamara's lot. The Buick-Pontiac King, John McNamara, had been taking advantage of the loose lending criteria of General Motors to secure loans to buy vans which he claimed to be customizing and selling overseas. At the height of the operation, had it actually existed, McNamara would have been churning out 400 customizations a day. Instead, he was operating a massive Ponzi scheme that took GM for $436 million.

What he did with the money sealed the Monarch's fate. Besides running a car dealership in the heart of Brookhaven Town, John McNamara was one of the area's biggest land developers and, by nature, a generous contributor to the powers that be. Despite community opposition, McNamara projects zoomed though the approval process and town board favors increased his profits many fold. In exchange for leniency, the Buick-Pontiac King provided a list of the officials he said he bribed, including the affable Don Zimmer. Some took plea bargains and left the town in disgrace, but Zimmer fought it tooth and nail. He was removed as councilman and ended up spending every penny he had defending himself. After a trial that laid bare the town's intricate relationship with shady characters such as John McNamara, Zimmer was found not guilty and was given a job as town senior citizens advocate to fill out his years.

Later in life I ran into him at town hall and deep worry overtook his jovial face.

"I'm dying of cancer, Bobby," he told me. "It was the smoking."

Shaking his hand for the last time, I noticed it was still yellow from tobacco. He smelled like a freshly extinguished pipe. I wondered to myself, *What the hell did he expect?*

CHAPTER 51

THE MONARCH TEETERS

The opposition had a field day with McNamara's connections to the Republicans and the Monarch went down in flames. It's the nature of politics to kick a man when he's down and it wasn't long before the Monarch's own club would keep the gossip mill churning.

Along the north shore of Long Island was a remarkable spit of land called West Meadow Beach that was lined with summer cottages and home to the Brookhaven Bathing Association Pavilion. It was here that the Monarchs hosted their annual luau, a well-attended event that served as an irritating burr between Mugsy's butt and his throne. Pouring rain greeted the guests, but under big white tents they would party on. At the end of the night, a club member commandeered a Budweiser beer trailer that served guests from six taps to keep the festivities going at his cottage down the beach. Backing it into his driveway, he hit a fire hydrant which preceded to wash out the street and drain off the water supply to the entire West Meadow peninsula.

Allow me to paraphrase the front-page story, featuring a huge headshot of the Monarch, that told the rest of the tale:

THREE MEN DIE AFTER MONARCH PARTY

Port Jefferson—Police searched for the bodies of three local men after their boat crashed into the jetty at the mouth of Port Jefferson Harbor following the Monarch Republican Club's annual beach party Friday night.

Drawn to pieces of a 21-foot boat among the rocks at the western entrance of the harbor, police found the body of Pat

King, 24, of Middle Island shortly after noon on Saturday. The rest of the boat was located at the bottom of the harbor and inside police divers found the remains of Scott Davis, 32, of Port Jefferson.

Known to be with the two men was Edwin Fox, 31, of Middle Island. He had not been located as of press time and is presumed dead.

Prior to crashing into the jetty, the men attended an annual luau party sponsored by the Monarch Republican Club at the Brookhaven Bathing Association at West Meadow Beach. Their families became alarmed when they did not return home and reported them missing.

Held in a driving rain storm, the Monarch Party was attended by local officials and judges. A Monarch board member hosted pre and post event parties at his West Meadow Beach cottage. The rain dampened a Grucci fireworks show scheduled for the evening.

After the Monarch bash, a Budweiser beer trailer knocked down a fence and damaged a fire hydrant while it was being backed into to the cottage for an after party. Attached to a water main, the hydrant broke open and cut off water to the 107 cottages on the peninsula. Flooding also cut off access to the cul-de-sac at the end of Trustees Road, according to a Setauket Fire Department fireman.

The president of the Monarch Club did not return calls seeking more information. It is unknown if the group had liability insurance to cover the damage.

A Port Jefferson Station businessman, the Monarch was president of the Port Jefferson Station/Terryville Chamber of Commerce and runs a glass shop with his family. He started the Monarch Club to raise funds for charities and support Republican candidates. He lost a race for Assemblyman Steven Englebright's old legislative seat to Democrat Nora Bredes.

CHAPTER 52

THE YOUNG BUCKS FALL

If being in the right place at the right time was a virtue, Mugsy was a virtuoso. As chairman of the GOP, Mugsy got to pick the candidate to run against High Tax Halpin and after floating a few names, settled on a little known assemblyman from his hometown. With Henny's tax attack still reverberating, Halpin got his clock cleaned and Mugsy took the credit. On the state level, an obscure senator by the name of George Pataki wanted to go up against the ever-popular Mario Cuomo for governor. Mugsy was one of his early supporters and Pataki won giving the former highway worker rock-star celebrity in the political world. Patronage and power would flow to Mugsy like manna from heaven.

Apparently, it wasn't enough. News that Mugsy was arrested by the feds for participating in an interstate chop shop ring for stolen trucks sent shock waves through the establishment. He defiantly denied the allegations and raked in money for a defense fund. After months of declaring his innocence, he pled guilty to everything from aiding and abetting the chop shop to collecting money from garbage haulers for illegal access to the town dump. He served two years in the federal pen and, after he was released to a halfway house, found himself back in the slammer for failing a drug test.

With Mugsy out of the picture, the Monarch's star was free to ascend and he became a key operative for Governor Pataki. As regional director of the state Office of General Services, the Monarch was responsible for all state buildings on Long Island

and New York City, where he maintained an office with a stunning view of the Empire State Building. Not to be outdone by Mugsy's fall from grace, however, the Monarch managed to get himself back into the headlines and this time, it was a doozy. If you put the world's best writers in a room and asked them to come up with a story to completely and utterly destroy a person's political career, they would come up with something like this, which appeared on the front page of the local paper with accompanying photo of the Monarch:

PROMINENT REPUBLICAN CHARGED IN ASSAULT

The ex-president of the Monarch Republican Club and former state official has been charged with assaulting a woman during the Republican National Convention held in New York City to re-nominate President George W. Bush for a second term.

According to the New York City Police Department, the Monarch was charged with assault in the third degree and unlawful imprisonment, both misdemeanors. The alleged incident occurred, police said, in a Manhattan apartment following a convention party the defendant and victim had attended.

The Monarch, 42, the ex-president of the Port Jefferson Station-Terryville Chamber of Commerce, denied the charges.

A local mother of two who requested that her name be withheld alleged the Monarch beat her in the apartment and refused to let her leave. He then forced her into his car and the two drove back to Long Island, she said, adding she was scared and wanted to get home to her children. Once they arrived in Port Jefferson, the woman said she drove herself to Mather Hospital.

According to Suffolk County police, who took a report based on the complaints, the woman was examined in the emergency room and was advised to file another report with the NYPD since the alleged assault happened in the city. The Monarch was issued a desk appearance ticket after the alleged victim told her story to city police.

"There was no arrest," the Monarch said, acknowledging there was a "personal issue" his attorneys are dealing with. "This is absolutely baseless and time will prove that out," he said. "Everyone has political enemies. My history will speak for itself." He said he did not hurt the complainant.

"As an ex-prosecuting attorney, my experience has been in these sorts of cases the circumstances are over charged," said the Monarch's attorney, Barry Zone. "He will not be convicted of a crime." Zone said there was no formal arrest and was confident the case would be "resolved quickly and without criminal consequences."

Police photos showed both the alleged victim's eyes swollen and blackened with cuts and scrapes above her upper lip and purple and yellow bruises showing in several places on her body, including her cheeks, neck, torso and thighs.

The Monarch had served as the director of the Office of General Services in charge of state buildings under Governor George Pataki. It's not clear when he left the job.

The alleged victim was willing to discuss the case in general terms, but not specific details since the investigation is continuing, saying she fears the Monarch could do the same to others.

"My thing is, he has children, he has two girls," she said. "He's had previous affairs. He's had to have done this before. Any other woman needs to know he is capable of doing this," she said adding, "People should know and he should get what he deserves."

She added that she and the defendant have known each other for many years and had been dating for the last two years. Both the Monarch and the alleged victim are married, but she said she is planning to divorce her husband.

The Monarch ran on the Republican ticket against Democrat Nora Bredes for the Suffolk County Legislature in 1992 and lost. The Comsewogue High School graduate helped start the Monarch Club, an organization that has promoted Republicans.

There was a time when I felt great sympathy for the Monarch. As a representative of Governor Pataki, he was called on to fill in for him at funerals and memorial services in the weeks following the terrorist attacks of 9/11 and the destruction of the World Trade Center. Unlike the governor who could breeze in, express his condolences, and leave, the Monarch had to sit there, sometimes for hours, and absorb all the grief and hysterics of the mourning families. Service after service, hour after hour, the heartbreak of fatherless children and widows and widowers in the wake of the most cataclysmic tragedy the nation has ever seen finally got to him. Through the course of a brief but rapid political career, surviving on his wits and charisma, the Monarch rose above and persevered. After 9/11, though nothing came of the charges against him, his star faded for good and his exit from the stage was, in its own right, tragic.

Making Andy Warhol proud, Mugsy and the Monarch had their 15 minutes of fame and then got scorched. At age 51, Mugsy was found dead in his bed, never recovering from his self-inflicted political wounds. The Monarch dropped out of sight, never to be heard from again. As for me, my political future was yet to be determined.

CHAPTER 53

SENATOR KENNEDY

Though he had been there before—the floor of the United States Senate—John was staggered by an overwhelming sense of awe as he entered the chamber. It was a place of immense history, the very building where his father served before he became president, and now he was entering the great hall not as a spectator, but as a participant, a senator of the United States of America.

John's uncle, Senator Edward Moore Kennedy, draped an arm around his shoulder.

"Welcome to the most exclusive club in the world."

John looked skyward and slowly scanned the ceiling from one side to the other to drink it all in. His family's history flooded through him starting with his father's oldest brother, Joseph Patrick Kennedy, Jr. *Correction,* John thought, *Lieutenant Joe Kennedy, Naval Aviator and hero of World War Two.*

John's uncle completed 25 missions flying an anti-submarine bomber and was eligible to return home. Instead, he volunteered to fly a secret mission, Operation Aphrodite, which would have him parachute from a plane loaded with explosives which would then be sent by remote control to its target, the Fortress of Mimoyecques in northern France. Minutes after the explosives were armed, the plane blew up over the North Sea, killing all aboard.

Joe Kennedy, the man groomed to be the first Irish Catholic President, was awarded the Distinguished Flying Cross, Air Medal, and the Navy Cross.

John had practically memorized his uncle's citation:

For extraordinary heroism and courage in aerial flight as pilot of a United States Liberator bomber on August 12, 1944. Well knowing the extreme dangers involved and totally unconcerned for his own safety, Kennedy unhesitatingly volunteered to conduct an exceptionally hazardous and special operational mission. Intrepid and daring in his tactics and with unwavering confidence in the vital importance of his task, he willingly risked his life in the supreme measure of service and, by his great personal valor and fortitude in carrying out a perilous undertaking, sustained and enhanced the finest traditions of the United States Naval Service.

John thought of his other uncle, Robert Francis Kennedy, also a senator from New York who was stuck down by an assassin after winning the California primary in his bid to become president. Uncle Bob was at the president's side when he stared down Khrushchev during the Cuban Missile Crisis and made it so that the first black student would attend the University of Mississippi.

John thought of his father, John Fitzgerald Kennedy. He did not remember the day he saluted him as a little boy, though the image was long etched in his mind. He hardly thought of it across his adult life, but on this day and this moment, the grainy footage replayed in his head.

"Come on, John, I want to show you something," his Uncle Ted led him down a carpeted isle. "Right here, at this spot," he said pointing. "This is where you father sat."

John was treated with reverence and respect as he began his work in the senate. He was named to the Budget Committee and a few subcommittees and though he couldn't control the legislative process directly, it seemed his colleagues, especially the leadership from both sides of the aisle, went out of their way to glean his comments and opinion. One thing he was happy to note was the problem with hysterical crowds died down since he made sure anyone who wanted to see him in person got a chance, albeit in large-scale venues. The rest of his meetings were mostly private affairs and many revolved around fundraising. He quickly became a prolific generator of money for the Democrat Party and its various action committees since no one, if asked, would turn him down.

CHAPTER 54

A TICKET OUT

One morning Henny asked me to attend a meeting on her behalf. Some "bigwigs" from Washington wanted to talk about putting a weather station in our town and thought it would be a good idea to touch base with the Supervisor's office. The group from DC was in a bind because the people of Islip, Brookhaven's neighbor to the west, were freaking out over the prospect of living next to a radar tower. The Washington folks made the mistake of announcing the site without laying any groundwork with local officials and supporters. When the Islip supervisor first got wind of the plan, it was from angry residents and naturally, he came out against it. At a community meeting to defend the project, the feds were greeted by mock graveyards and Grim Reapers with scythes saying if the radar was built, it would kill the people living around it. The backup plan was to put it at the Brookhaven National Lab.

I told the Washington contingent that if they do what they did in Islip here in Brookhaven, I would run them out of town. Coming to see Supervisor Acampora was a good first step, I said, but Long Island is a land of politicians and if you don't go hat in hand to each and every one of them, in addition to the not-in-my-back-yard civic associations and other pot stirrers, it would only take one crusader to pull the plug. They were all ears. I suggested they get a hold of the farmers and fishermen who would benefit from better weather reports, as well as trade unions and chambers of commerce that would appreciate the jobs and other benefits the multi-million installation would bring. They asked me for a list of people they should go see and I rattled off a dozen or so names with phone numbers still fresh in my mind from my days as a reporter. They were impressed.

A few weeks after they left, I got a call for advice. The Affiliated Brookhaven Civic Organizations, an umbrella group of civics, and the East Yaphank Civic Association were meeting on the same night and because they only had one person in town, wanted to know which meeting to go to. It would seem the best bet would be to meet with the larger group, the affiliates, but I told them to go to Yaphank, the group nearest to the proposed site.

The meeting kicked off with the usual Pledge of Allegiance, treasurer's report, old business, etc. and then went to the topic of the weather station. They politely introduced the man from Washington, part of the group of three that had been to Henny's office that day, and right off the bat a local resident lit into him. He started to regale the crowd with stories of graveyards and grim reapers, but before he could get too far, an elderly lady sitting next to me jumped up and cut him off.

"I worked with radars for 30 years and can tell you right now they're safe and we should welcome them," the lady said, staring directly at the griping man. "I make a motion to support the National Weather Service and their facility."

"Second."

"All in favor."

"Aye."

"Those against." The griper froze.

"There being none, the motion is passed and carried."

The Washington man was dumbfounded. A few days later I faxed him a front page article from Suffolk Life: "Civic Group Supports Weather Service."

The people who had come to the Supervisor's office—the Director of the National Weather Service, the Director of the Weather Service Eastern Region, and the one who attended the meeting, the National Director of Public Affairs—were ecstatic.

Every year, the Republicans lose big in the area around Stony Brook University, a magnet for liberal Democrats. When I registered to vote as a student at Oswego College, my application was forwarded to Suffolk County where they enrolled me to vote. It happens different now. Stony Brook students are encouraged to enroll and vote locally because the Democrats know they lean their way.

As president of the Young Republican Club, I was approached by a man named Bond, director of the Republican National Committee, to see what I could do to help turn the tide. The Republican candidate for congress lost by thousands of votes, many coming from the university, and if the GOP wanted to ever win the seat, they needed to neutralize Stony Brook. I hooked up with the College Republican Club, four young men in total, and got Bond to give them scholarships of $500 each. Where you once had zero Republican activity on campus, you now had four guys out there hustling and in the next congressional race, we evened out the tally.

Bond was impressed and when he learned a job was opening up with the federal government on Long Island, he gave me a call. After five years in the political trenches of Brookhaven Town, I was worn out and disgusted and itching for a change. The job was with the National Weather Service and I was interviewed by my three friends from Washington. They wanted me to help them situate the rest of their weather facilities in the northeast and I joined on as the new Public Affairs Specialist for the National Weather Service Eastern Region.

Ten years went by fast and the weather service modernization was practically done. The job was getting dull. Plus, I was sick of occupying the cubicle next to the grossest man on earth. "Bumpy" had these weird growths popping out all over his body, including his face, but that wasn't the problem. Every day at lunch he would eat franks and beans, Ruben sandwiches, stuffed cabbage and any other odiferous food he could think of and spent the afternoon farting and burping like he was at a frat party. Every time he would let one rip, he would disguise the noise by clearing his throat, but this didn't fool anyone since his sulfuric aroma would waft into my work space like a London fog. Complaining to management got me nowhere and whenever I brought it up to Bumpy, he blamed it on the food he ate. "Well for Christ's sake," I told him, "don't eat that kind of food."

The cubicle mate opposite us was no help either. He was the EEO guy, Equal Employment Opportunity, and I guess he felt the government should have at least one disgusting person in every office. His name was something like Joe Smith and one day announced himself as Hassan Sulaiman and started wearing a strange hat. Shortly after that, he left. I think he went undercover for the CIA.

I can't complain too much about that office since it was where I met my wife. We had a mischievous matchmaker in our midst who asked me what I thought of the beautiful Asian lady in admin. I said I thought she was nice and the next thing I know she comes into my cubicle and gives me a big hug. We were married not too long after.

CHAPTER 55

PULLED BACK IN

John described George as a "lifestyle magazine with politics at its core, illuminating the points where politics converges with business, media, entertainment, fashion, art and science. Whether it's violence in the movies or free speech on the Internet, culture drives politics. The public arena is not a hothouse sealed off from the general climate," he told his readers. "It partakes of it, changes it, and is changed by it."

And John, if I may add, politics will disrupt your life. It will grab you, shake you and use you up. If you're lucky, it will spit you out no better or worse than you were before. If you're lucky.

It was a Saturday afternoon when I received another life-altering call and this time it was Senator LaValle's cousin, the new supervisor of the Town of Brookhaven, John Jay LaValle. He wanted to know if I was interested in joining his administration as Commissioner of Parks. After sitting through countless government meetings quite convinced I could do a better job than the clowns running the show, and after years of flacking to fulfill the ambitions of others, I would finally get to see how I could run something.

As commissioner, I would be in charge of a hundred full-time employees, dozens more in the summer, and responsible for dozens of parks, pools, beaches, buildings, and other town facilities, including marinas, docks, cemeteries, nature preserves, and the old town hall where I spent my early days with Don Zimmer, Henrietta and the crew. I would oversee major construction projects, renovations, recreation programs, and budgets in the millions. John

Jay said he was serious about correcting the crap that went on before us and I felt confident we could make some changes for the better.

I accepted the challenge and the following month, was in the audience at the town's organizational meeting, the first session of the year where appointments and new business were settled. I was resolution #76, fourth from the bottom, and was unanimously approved by the town board. As the meeting broke up, my eye was caught by Councilman Dominic Santoro coming down off the dais. I nodded politely and quickly realized he was locked onto me like a laser. I watched him wend through the crowd, not once taking his eyes off me. Surely he had no beef with me, especially since I helped him in his reelection. In fact, I drew up the nominating petition he used to get on the ballot.

I'll never forget this because it was the day my daughter was born. Meerah was scheduled for a C-section and I brought her to the hospital in the morning. Unlike other husbands who want to be there for every gory moment, Meerah was okay with me hiding out in the waiting room. I sat there for a few minutes and thought, *This was going to take a while,* so I shot over to Republican headquarters to finish up Santoro's petition.

I ran into the party treasurer, Dickman, who was in a tizzy because someone ordered a letter folding machine without consulting him. He thought he was a big power broker by virtue of his position on the town's Zoning Board of Appeals and when he found out I was the culprit, starting railing at me like I was his peon. Right when I was about to tell him to go blank himself, one of the town board members came in, wrote out a check to cover the purchase, and gave him a look that basically said, "Shut the hell up you big blow hard."

Like the percussionist who shows up at the end of the symphony to bang the gong, I waltzed back into the waiting room just as the nurse came out to present me with our precious new gift. It was the first time I ever held a baby and the proud papa was beaming. In the days leading up to the delivery, I tore a muscle in my butt kicking a soccer ball (for the first time in years) and it threw my back out of kilter so bad I could hardly walk. That night, after visiting mom and the newborn, I had to spend a few minutes laying in the hallway to work up enough tolerance to the pain to find my way out. My path led me to a door and I limped through it to the outside. Instead of the parking lot, I found myself in a fenced-in utility area, the door locking behind me. No one was in sight and I spent the remaining hours of the day laying on the grass, contemplating what the future would bring. I was still in pain 19 days later when the terrorists attacked the World Trade Center. Had I not heeded President Kennedy's call and chose the Wall Street route instead of public service, would I have been working for Euro Brokers like my high school friend Bill Matheson who died in the South Tower?

"Fire Heart Attack," were the first words out of Councilman Santoro's mouth after he waded through the crowd to reach me. "The first thing I want you to do is get rid of him."

"Okay," I replied, not having a clue who or what he was talking about. My answer pleased him immensely and he walked away smiling.

My first days on the job were a whirlwind of briefings and meetings and before the week was through, I got a call from the man himself, Heart Attack. Turns out he worked for a company that did consulting work for the town. The workers hated him and made sure I knew they weren't too happy about a letter from the previous administration directing the staff to answer to Heart Attack as if he were the commissioner. He wanted to come see me and a date was set. In the meantime, my secretary threw open the door of a nearby office to reveal Heart Attack's refuge, a veritable shrine of plaques, photos with big shot Republicans and Democrats alike, and a most curious assemblage of miniature collectables lining the window sills. The room was immaculate.

I must say I was anxious to meet Mr. Heart Attack, particularly for him to discuss the various projects the employees described as disasters. One job was the renovation of a town pool where, when they turned on the pumps, saw water boil up through the concrete decking. A forensic engineer was brought in to dig up the mess and it was easy to figure out why it was leaking. Instead of carefully packed sand, pieces of the old deck were thrown in to cover the new work. We found a piece of concrete with red paint that used to spell out the pool's depth, "4 feet," sticking out of the main return. Valves wouldn't hold water in the pump room and the new concrete was cracking. Instead of the specified six inches, it was only four inches thick. The job cost the taxpayers millions and even more to fix.

Over at the Cedar Beach life guard tower, the walls sprouted black mold thanks to new windows that leaked and holes punched through the roof where a new deck was nailed on. I quickly learned that screwing the town was the name of the game and it seemed like everyone was in on the action. When six foot trees were ordered, three footers showed up and I was told tales of truckloads of top soil ordered to remote locations only to be hauled away by landscapers, contractors, and whoever else was in on the scam. The workers never seemed to have the right equipment because every year there would be a "surplus" auction where the good stuff would sell off for a song. Material and machines would frequently disappear and I wondered if there was a guy somewhere with a barn full of rakes, shovels, gloves, fertilizer—you name it—that would never see the light of day.

Oil burners were forever on the fritz—on purpose—since each time the repairman was called, he would whack the town for a few hundred bucks. When we finally got rid of him the new guy pointed out that at each location there was a supply of the nozzles needed to shoot the oil into the burner. The problem was they were the wrong size and guaranteed to clog after a month or two. So the schemer would cash in each time he changed them out.

After a few invoices crossed my desk for landscape maintenance at the town's cemeteries, we went out to take a look. Turns out they were almost completely overgrown with the only mowing being a path down the middle.

At the marinas, contractors installed the wrong type of piping knowing full well it would leak and a new round of overspending would ensue to fix it. Another classic was the permit game where the consultants would design environmental projects they knew the state would never approve and hit the cash register each time they had to revise the plans.

A call from the state retirement system clued us in on why the paint at most of the facilities was peeling off. The town employed two full-time painters who thought it would be okay to pad their pensions by working second jobs—during the hours they were supposed to be painting for the town.

Working in an environment like this, the employees were unproductive to say the least and before I got there, filed grievances for violations of the union contract about every week.

The work ethic went something like this:

Foreman: "The grass is really high in the front of the rec center. Get it cut."

Crew Leader: "No problem."

Foreman (a few days later): "The grass is only cut in the front. What about the back?"

Crew Leader: "You didn't say anything about the back."

The portfolio of scams, schemes, and second-rate work went on and on and had a horrible effect on the shape of the parks system. I was chomping at the bit to hear Heart Attack's side of the story. The day of our meeting finally came, but he was nowhere to be found. That night at a fundraiser hosted by the Supervisor I was approached by a man who kissed me on the cheek. It was the chief honcho at Heart Attack's firm who said he looked forward to working with me. I told him his company wasn't getting off to a very good start, letting him know his main man didn't bother to show up for our meeting.

The next morning kicked off with Heart Attack on the phone ranting and raving about me making him look bad to his boss. I referenced the missed meeting and he said he would be right over. He never showed up. On the third attempt, he called to say he would be a little late and called again saying he would be there shortly. He never made it and if he did, he would have found all of his stuff waiting for him by the door.

Councilman Santoro, the town board liaison to the department of parks, envisioned a grand renovation of the Bald Hill Amphitheater, Brookhaven's former ski bowl that was transformed into a huge open-air concert venue. He wanted dressing rooms, office space, and other amenities that would attract big acts to Brookhaven. This was in the wake of the Eddie Fall fiasco, a promoter the town hired who sold tickets to shows, cancelled them, and pocketed the money. The town was attempting to make the amphitheater a success, with the councilman as the point man, but it seems Heart Attack butted heads with him until a new commissioner came in and that was that.

Under the old system, most projects died on the drawing board and the few that did move forward were deemed "clusterfucks" by the staff. The consultants loved large, complicated projects because they got paid for the design, eating up the budget and not giving a crap if the thing ever got built. You can see the result today at the town's ballparks where you have fields facing out from a central point where a scoring tower was supposed to be with bathrooms and storage. With the money burned up in the planning phase, all you have left is empty space and smelly porta-potties.

According to the prevailing wisdom, the schemers got away with it because they donated to the party in power. Over at Republican headquarters, I got a look at the books and found that the money coming in had no bearing on who got away with what. Either people were getting pretty well greased under the table or the whole operation was so incompetent that nobody noticed or even cared.

Given the chance, the employees argued, they could rebuild the parks system a lot faster than the existing set up and save a ton of money. Maybe it was time to see what they could do.

CHAPTER 56

MORE JOHN

Enough already, I was told one afternoon at the bar. Harvard was back and Big Daddy and Sandra—all a little older and wiser—and I had picked up some new fans. The stories about my life were "interesting," I was told, but everyone wanted more John.

Okay, here goes:

A day came that would change the world. Senator Kennedy was at his office on Third Avenue in New York City when he was told that a plane had crashed into one of the twin towers at the World Trade Center. He went to the window and could see smoke in the distance. On the conference room TV flames billowed from an ugly black gash in the massive South Tower, one of the tallest structures in the world. With television cameras from every network in the media capital of the world now focused on the matching buildings, people did not yet realize the nation was under attack.

And then another plane appeared and John watched helplessly as an orange fireball tore through the North Tower and exploded out the other side.

"I have to get down there," he said to his staff.

John was on his bicycle still in his suit and dodged people and traffic streaming out of lower Manhattan. He pedaled toward the two rising plumes of smoke and though he was in very good shape, was winded by the exertion.

"Where do you think you're going, Champ?" a burly cop stopped him at a police barricade on Chambers Street.

"I'm Senator Kennedy. I have to get down to the Trade Center."

"Not on my watch you ain't. Those buildings are burning. Not a safe place to be."

John turned his bike around and headed back up Broadway. Pedaling furiously, sometimes down the middle of the road, John crossed over on Reade Street toward the river. He would make an end run at Greenwich and approach the Trade Center from the west. At Barclay, he ditched his bike and loosened his tie. There was a roadblock, but the scene was chaos with the police trying to guide people out of the financial center. He slipped though and was one of the very few walking against the grain toward the burning buildings. Flames shot from the wounds where the planes sliced through and they encroached into the floors above. People hung out of windows waving white garments. Even so high above, John could see them tortured from the heat and smoke.

Suddenly, a woman jumped and John followed her path down to the street. People shrieked and the wail of sirens echoed through the canyon. Then John felt an eerie rumble that stopped him dead in his tracks. The walls below the flames started to crumble and then the square top of the roof shifted and like a giant anvil crushed down on the floors below. The South Tower was coming down.

John watched it fall, but for only a second, and then he started running, the deep growl of the collapse following behind. He ducked between two cars just as the cyclone overtook him, a white storm of heat, pellets and ash. It blew past him for an eternity and sucked the air from his lungs. He forced in a breath only to fill his throat with dust and he began choking.

So this is how it's going to end, Old Sport, he thought as snippets of his life flashed before him. There was Carolyn in her blond radiance and his mother lounging on a sandy beach. He saw the Capitol Building dome lit up like a bright beacon on a hill and watched a scratchy movie of a little boy in a powder blue suit.

"Buddy, are you okay?"

John opened his eyes to a white ghost.

"Come on, we gotta get out of here."

John coughed and a cloud of dust like talcum powder shot from his mouth. He gasped and it hurt to draw back in. The man, covered in ash with blood-red eyes and hair blown back, grabbed his arm and pulled him up.

"This way."

The street was sandblasted white and deathly quiet. A few other people staggered along with them, kicking up small clouds of dust as they went.

From a side street, a man with a camera appeared and snapped a photo that would set in stone the horror of 9/11 and the power of man's spirit to live. A moment before, John's savior had fallen to his knees and John pulled him up. It was John walking the stranger through the hellacious smoke and debris that the world would see, not the man saving John. The picture appeared on the front page of every newspaper and was part of every newscast even before they figured out that the blast-beruffled figure carrying his fellow man to safety was indeed, The Prince of Camelot.

The pair staggered to an aide station set up between two ambulances. EMT's grabbed them and pushed them onto waiting stretchers. John faded in and out of consciousness, the only thing keeping him awake was his overriding need to cough. A team wheeled him to another ambulance waiting in a line to take the survivors away. Then they froze in their tracks. John's stretcher began to vibrate and the whole world shook. The second tower was coming down. The rescue team threw their bodies over him as a tornado of white wind blasted through like the wash of a jet engine. Fortunately, they were far enough away to avoid the brunt of the collapse and quickly loaded the freshly-dusted John into the ambulance.

Around the corner, not too far away, the place where John fell and contemplated the end of his life, was obliterated.

CHAPTER 57

THE HEAT IS...OFF

At my desk in the department of parks I measured the paperwork in feet. A half a foot would be the norm for a day, but often the stack would be higher. The commissioner's signature was required on all matters of departmental business and I scrutinized everything that landed in my box. A particular item caught my eye: the contract with the town's new heating oil company. Being it was the dead of winter, I asked my executive assistant, Wayne, to make sure there weren't any problems with the transition.

Despite his best efforts, the ensuing days were a fiasco with various senior citizen centers, park offices, and other buildings without heat.

"What happened?" I wanted to know.

"The new driver couldn't find all of the locations and didn't fill the tanks," said my exasperated assistant.

"Get with him and make sure he fills them all," I told him.

The next morning, more calls—no heat.

"Some of the locations have different tanks for different burners and he didn't know they were there," came the explanation.

The next morning, no heat.

"The gate was locked and he couldn't get in."

The next morning, no heat, and making matters worse there was a repeat outage at a senior center and the director, a real barracuda, was on the warpath.

"Don't worry, I'll make sure everyone stays warm," I assured her.

"You better."

"Wayne, I don't care if you have to fill the tanks yourself, make sure everyone has heat."

"Yes, boss."

A few days later, no heat at the senior center, and the Barracuda is livid, threatening to go to the newspapers.

"What the hell happened?"

"Someone left the back door open and the furnace ran all weekend. Burned up all the oil."

"Shit."

Next morning, no heat, and the Barracuda tried to get me fired.

"The driver quit and they had to hire a new one."

Next morning, no heat.

"It snowed and nobody plowed by the tanks."

"It was the end of the day and his truck was empty."

"Someone ran into the cap and he couldn't get it off."

"They couldn't get the burner working again after the oil ran out."

It reminded me of the Blues Brothers movie where John Belushi as Joliet Jake comes up with one excuse after another for ditching his bride at the altar:

I ran outta gas.

I had a flat tire.

I didn't have enough money for cab fare.

My tux didn't come back from the cleaners.

An old friend came in from outta town.

Someone stole my car.

There was an earthquake.

A terrible flood.

Locusts.

It wasn't my fault, I swear to God!

"Sorry Wayne," I told him, "you can't use any of those."

The poor guy went to every site, made maps, typed up directions, and watched the weather forecasts like a hawk. I think he even drove around with a couple of five gallon tanks of heating oil in his trunk just to make sure. He was suicidal.

This went on for weeks until one morning, no calls. "Holy crap, Wayne! I think you did it."

"Un-fucking believable."

Wayne did give me a good laugh once when he reported a freshly dug grave at one of the town's historic cemeteries, a place that hadn't seen a burial in a century. "What do you think we should do?" I asked him.

"Let 'em rest in peace."

CHAPTER 58

ESCAPE

John woke up to a beeping noise and focused his eyes on the bland room around him. Wires rose up from his body and connected to a monitor with jagged lines moving across the screen. A clear tube went from his arm to a bag hanging on a hook and liquid dripped into it. He felt his heart beat along with the spikes in the monitor.

I gotta get back to the Trade Center.

A nurse came in to catch him swinging his legs over the side of the bed.

"Not so fast, Mr. Kennedy," the snow-white angel said as she gently pushed him back onto the bed.

"What hospital am I in?" A spasm of coughs hit him as he spoke.

"New York Downtown."

"How long have I been here?"

"Since yesterday. Do you know what happened?"

John thought for a second. "The tower went down. It collapsed. Do you know how many people were killed?"

"It was both towers. Both towers came down."

The Senator shook his head in disbelief. "And the dead?"

"Don't worry about that now, Mr. Kennedy. Please sit back. Rest."

John stared at the wires, stunned.

"I have to get back there. I have to help."

"Not right now you're not."

"Okay. But when can I go?"

"That'll be up to the doctors," the nurse told him. "For now, please get some rest and I'll check in with you a little later."

Outside John's room was a frenzy of activity. Victims of the attack were lined up in the halls on stretchers and wheelchairs. Doctors and nurses flashed by, a fireman clanked through in full gear.

I gotta get out of here.

The Senator followed the plastic tube to his arm and peeled off the tape that held it. It bristled with black hair. The IV needle slid out and John hung it next to the clear bag. For the wires, he had to act quickly. The first one was embedded in his chest and it stung when he pulled it. He tore off the next one and the monitor flat lined with a piercing beep. He slapped off the ones on his wrists and ankles and now he was free.

John merged into the traffic streaming through the hallway and felt like a sore thumb in his light blue gown tied in the back. He passed by rooms that held four and five stretchers and was annoyed that they gave him his own room. John went for the stairs instead of the elevator and, looking back as the door closed, could see the nurse rushing toward his room. He thought he was pretty clever grabbing a plastic bag with his wallet, watch and cellphone as he made his escape.

Out on the street, he called his most trusted aide, Shawn Smith, a hard-worker put on his staff by the Four Men.

"Glad to hear your voice," the aide said. "Now don't move a muscle. Carolyn is on her way and I'm right behind her."

"I'm not at the hospital."

"What do you mean you're not at the hospital?"

"I left. I have to get back to the Trade Center."

"Are you nuts?

"Meet me at Beekman and William. How soon can you be there?"

"I'm right by City Hall. Just a few minutes. I'm getting through the checkpoints pretty quick with my senate ID."

Smith wrapped his boss in a bear hug. "We didn't know if you were dead or alive," the aide told him. "It wasn't easy finding you, but once we found out it was downtown, we were on our way."

"Do you have any of my clothes?" John said, running his hands down his chest to show off his dainty hospital wear.

"In the trunk," said the aide who made it a habit of carrying a few outfits for the man who was constantly on the go.

John grabbed a polo shirt, khaki pants and the only choice available, black socks. He wriggled out of the blue outfit in the passenger seat of Smith's car and into the civilian clothes. He looked down at his aide's feet.

"Shawn, I need you to do me a big favor," John coughed as he spoke. "I need you to give me your shoes."

"Senator, are you okay? I don't like that cough. What did they say when you left the hospital?"

"They didn't say anything."

"The doctors didn't say anything about your condition?"

"I didn't exactly talk to them. Now, the shoes, please."

Smith pulled off his black Nikes and squeezed into a shiny pair of wing tips from the trunk.

"What are you going to do at the Trade Center? The place is in ruins. It's still on fire. What are you going to do there?"

"Anything I can."

Smith drove the Senator through an increasingly difficult series of road blocks and at the last one, at a corner bleached white with dust and clogged with debris, they could go no further.

The Senator jumped from the car. "Tell Carolyn I'm okay," he called out. "Tell her I love her."

John backtracked to a familiar route, and was again heading up Reade toward Greenwich. The dust padded his steps and he move silently, stopping every few minutes to catch his breath and clear his lungs with deep, painful hacks.

"I'm Senator Kennedy," he said to the officer at an impenetrable blockade at Vesey Street.

"Sorry, no one gets in here."

The Senator pulled his ID from his wallet. "I'm Senator John F. Kennedy. I need to get in."

"Sorry."

The exchange caught the attention of a higher up standing nearby.

"Guy says he's Senator Kennedy," the cop reported. "Needs to get to the pile."

The superior officer eyeballed him.

"I'll be damned. Senator Kennedy. Pleased to meet you, sir," the officer said as he reached out to shake John's hand.

"Billy, let him through."

The barricade was moved and John stared at the collapsed gates of hell.

"Senator," Billy spoke up. "Here, take this." He gave John a New York City Police Department cap.

John walked slow, barely able to comprehend what he was seeing. Men with hoses shot water onto giant mounds glowing with flames. Dense plumes of black smoke swirled into the sky and he could hardly see through the haze that enveloped the scene. When the plumes of smoke shifted he could make out piles of ruin reaching many stories high. He recognized the crisscross pattern of the tower's façade in a broken lattice that rose up from a huge mound of smoldering concrete. Workers moved frantically among the wreckage using their hands to remove debris piece by piece in a long human chain.

"Quiet. Quiet everyone," a man yelled over a bullhorn. The pile fell deathly silent as handlers clamped their hands over the muzzles of agitated rescue dogs. "If you can hear us, bang on something. A pipe, metal. Bang as hard as you can."

A thousand ears listened.

"Bang if you can hear us."

A tap! From deep within a mountain of rubble, the rescuers heard a tap.

"We hear you," the man with the bullhorn yelled. "We are coming."

The workers started in again with a new burst of urgency. John joined the chain and a rush of power coursed through his body as he passed pieces of broken concrete down the line.

Like everyone around him, John coughed into the dusty air, not bothering to cover his mouth with his dirty hands. After one particularly violent outburst, he dropped to one knee and the workers adjusted to fill his spot on the line.

An arm went around his shoulder and guided him over to a makeshift aid station where they gave him water and a wet cloth to wipe his face.

"Please," John said in a low voice, looking down at the broken ground, embarrassed. "A pair of gloves," he asked. "Can I trouble you for a pair of gloves?"

"Here," the man said, "and what are you doing without a mask?"

John got back on the line, his hands throbbing through the gloves. He appreciated the mask and his coughing fits came less frequent.

"Quiet," the man with the bullhorn only had to say it once. The team dropped silent, grateful for the respite.

The tapping was much louder now. They were closing in.

John found himself at the front of the line picking up stony pieces and shoving them toward the hands behind him. A group of five swarmed in to muscle a fragment too big for John to handle. They tipped it away and it slid down the pile nearly hitting a man below.

"An arm. There's an arm," John cried out as a dozen hands scratched the rubble to set it free. They exposed a shoulder, then a head that was protected in a small pocket where two pieces of concrete had tee-peed together. They pulled the man free, broken but alive.

Practically holding his breath as they freed the man, John burst out in another ferocious round of coughing. He wiped his mouth with the wet cloth from his pocket and drew it away smeared with blood.

"That's enough for today, son," a large man in a fire department jacket told him as he led him down the hill away from the pile. John was passed to another set of arms which walked him to the checkpoint.

"No re-admittance," the man commanded as the guards nodded with reverence.

CHAPTER 59

SAVED A LIFE

Spring was upon us so I set about visiting every town park to see what needed to be done. I created a spreadsheet and listed everything from the park name, location, size and features such as playgrounds, ball fields, pools, bathrooms and docks, as well as what would be needed to renovate and maintain them. In Heart Attack's old office there was a blueprint machine that used a roll of paper three feet wide. When we printed the list, it rolled out 10-feet long. I included a special column, "All Bald," to check off parks that didn't have any grass left, just dirt and weeds. Ironically, many of the All Balds had sprinkler systems that didn't work. The answer why was as obvious as it was painful: "If you grow grass you have to cut it."

Over at the Mastic Rec Center, the façade was rotting off the side of the building and the interior looked like hell. I asked the maintenance supervisor why. "We could never get the supplies to do anything," he told me. "So we stopped asking."

Since the town's inception in 1655, the people of Brookhaven elected their council members "at large," meaning they could vote for each of the six representatives and these officials answered to all. Being that a majority of the voters were Republican, the Democrats didn't stand a chance of getting elected town wide, so they pushed a plan to divide Brookhaven into ward districts. With elections now in specific areas they could focus their energies where there were pockets of Democrat voters and possibly win a seat. The new scheme was put before the people in a referendum and they agreed. Now you had council members actually caring about the parks in their particular districts and the pressure was on to undo years of what the old system had wrought.

Every park has a Mayor, a frequent visitor or neighbor who keeps an eye on the place and wants to know why it's not better taken care of. In the at-large system, the Mayors got shuffled around until they gave up. With the ward system, they knew exactly who to call and in turn, those officials called the commissioner.

West Meadow Beach with its stunning views of the Long Island Sound and Connecticut in the distance is one of the crown jewels of the parks system and, befitting its status, had an ambitious advocate who refused to accept the status quo. The Mayor of West Meadow demanded I meet him at the park and I arrived with clipboard in hand. Take a closer look at this beautiful beach and it was easy to see what was bugging him. Weeds grew up through cracks in the parking lot and sand piled up against the curbs. Debris littered the seashore and rotting park benches sat off kilter. The pavilion needed a new roof and the bathrooms didn't have hot water. Toilets and urinals had plastic bags taped over them—out of order—and the pulley on the flag pole rusted off so they couldn't raise a flag. A gazebo sat dilapidated.

Perturbing the Mayor most of all was instead of toilet paper holders, the bathrooms featured iron bars with padlocks to secure the rolls so no one would steal them. To the user's great dismay the bars were too wide and the rolls didn't roll so when you were sitting there in need, you had to pull off one little square at a time.

"Do you realize how ridiculous this is?" the Mayor asked, wanting to know what kind of management system produces such poor results. I knew the answer to that one and shared the explanation I was given by the union brass my first week on the job.

"Let's say you could get a job for someone, anyone, that is well paying with full benefits, health insurance, Cadillac retirement plan, and they don't really have to work that hard," I said to him. "They'll have a truck to take home and get plenty of overtime. Who would you hire?"

The Mayor thought it over. "Someone who works hard and deserves a good job."

"Hell no," I was told. "You'd hire your sister's deadbeat husband who hasn't held down a steady job in his life."

"I see."

"So now this guy with the political connections is making more money than he ever did without having to do very much. Do you think he's happy?"

The Mayor pondered the question.

"No way!" I answered for him. "Because he sees another guy working even less, but is making more, and that really pisses him off. In fact, he makes it a point to do even less and bitch and moan until he gets away with what the other guy gets away with."

"Hell of a way to run a railroad."

"Wait, it gets better."

"When it comes time to promote crew leaders and foremen, who do you think they pick?"

"The people who work the hardest with the most ability?"

"You wish. Promotions are based on seniority. The guy who's been around longer moves up."

"So the ones who have perfected the art of doing the least amount of work get the promotions?"

"Exactly. And do you think the guys under him appreciate it? No way, and the cycle of misery continues."

"Wow."

"So now you know the secrets of creating a dysfunctional system."

After I got fired I met up with the Mayor at West Meadow for old time's sake. We saw a parks department truck winding toward us and even then, I knew the lone driver wasn't where he was supposed to be. I decided to have a little fun.

"Mr. Mayor, when he gets here, ask him what he did today."

"Okay."

"But don't let him off the hook easy. Keep asking and you'll get the Five Stages of Denial, sort of like the coping mechanism for loss and grief. Are you game?"

"Sure."

Me: "Sheppy, how the hell are you? Long time no see."

Sheppy: "I'm doing great, Commissioner. Good to see you."

Me: "You know the Mayor?"

Sheppy: "How ya doin?"

Mayor: "So, what have you been up to?"

Sheppy: "Oh, the usual. Same old, same old."

Mayor: "Like what?"

Sheppy: "Working pretty hard."

Mayor: "Doing what, exactly?"

Sheppy: "Doing more than the other guys, that's for sure."

Mayor: "Like what?"

Sheppy: "Breaking my ass and nobody freaking appreciates it, that's what."

Mayor: "Honestly, what specifically have you done today?"

Sheppy: "Doing my job, man. Breaking my ass."

Mayor: "Are you working here or somewhere else?"

Sheppy: "I'm working all over the place."

Mayor: "Where?"

Sheppy: "You know, here and there."

Mayor: "Doing what?"

Sheppy (storming off): "I don't have to put up with this shit. Screw you."

Mayor: "Amazing!"

"The truth is," I said as Sheppy drove off, "he hasn't done anything all day, probably all week."

"Unbelievable. Why don't they fire him?"

"Would take a court order and could you imagine what the rest of them would do if you cracked down on one of their own?"

I continued, "The sad part is that avoiding work all day is harder than actually doing it, has a terrible effect on the psyche. The town would save a lot on gas if they could just send them someplace to hide."

"Yet, you got things done," the Mayor said. "West Meadow got fixed up. There's hot water and a new roof and toilet paper rolls that work. The flag pole was even fixed. How'd you do it?"

"Something I learned from Bill Clinton."

When I worked for the weather service, the president came up with the idea of a Union-Management Partnership. He asked our agency what he could expect from us and what we needed to get it done. I did the same thing with the parks union. I had the list of what needed to be done and asked them how much of it they could handle. They knew what the overtime budget was and how much we could spend on materials and equipment. The bottom line was I didn't care how they got it done and I wouldn't be breathing down their necks. I didn't care who goofed off and who didn't. But the deal was, whatever they said they would do, they had to do it and whatever was left on the list, I could use outside contractors without the union putting up a stink.

They agreed.

With a partnership between the employees and a commissioner who actually cared, the department flourished. The lunatics were put in charge of the asylum, so to speak, and God bless them, they kept their word. When things got done, I made sure the credit went to the workers and the various Mayors jumped at the chance to give them a pat on the back. The elected officials held their heads high with their constituents for promises fulfilled. They even listed our projects in their election brochures.

The employees started having pride in their work and it showed. They still screwed up from time to time and I went to bat for them when they did. They appreciated it when I put on work clothes and joined them in the field. I liked getting out from behind the desk and picked up trash and planted beach grass and trees right along with them. I still go out of my way sometimes to visit the parks I worked on to admire their growth. For the projects not on the union list, we used the outside contractors and made sure they did the job right without ripping us off.

We tackled some big jobs that would normally be drawn-out money pits courtesy of Heart Attack and his ilk. At the top of the list was the Wedge, a triangular piece of land at the confluence of two major roads where public outrage blocked the building of a Home Depot. The town took over the 18-acre site in a deal with the developer and the pressure was on to turn it into a park. The union lined up the town's bulldozers and excavators and went to work. The result was a rolling complex of hills and fields, playgrounds and walking paths that is appreciated by many, particularly the men and women who built it "in-house" and saved the taxpayers a fortune.

The construction of another facility, Osprey Park, was already underway when I got there and the project was vexed by setbacks and money issues. The plumbing contractor was all over me because he bid on the job not realizing the "Jumping Jewels" kiddie sprinkler system called for in the plans would cost him $18,000, pretty much his entire profit. I wouldn't let him off the hook.

The general contractor was after me for $30,000 in extra decking he said wasn't called for in the specs. I wouldn't give it to him. He was also dogged by a rash of vandalism that started the day materials were first delivered to the site. We caught the kid, a local teen, and it was up to me as to whether the town would press charges. I set up a meeting with him and his parents. I could have had the kid start off his life with a criminal record, but what would that have accomplished? I'm sure his friends would continue wrecking the place and his ultimate payback for ruining his life probably would have been a doozy. I had a better idea.

"Why don't you come work for us?" I said to the kid who looked baffled, though his father got it right away.

"You can be the night watchman, earn a couple of bucks, or you can go to court. Your choice."

I didn't have to explain myself twice and from then on, we had no trouble at the park, except for the Jumping Jewels, which never worked right.

CHAPTER 60

SAVED A LIFE

John trudged through the white powder toward Barclay thinking about something he saw at the pile: a sturdy iron cross made from the intersection of two beams standing among the chaos. John and the men were inspired by it, yet wondered how a God that's great and good could permit such devastation and death.

Holy shit, wow! he thought upon seeing his bicycle still leaning up against a signpost, exactly where he left it. He took off for TriBeCa. At a small incline, he had to stop pedaling and walked his bike the rest of the way up Church Street. He felt like he was going to die, yet a terrific elation ran through him. *I helped save a man's life!*

Carolyn buzzed him in and met him in the hall.

"Goddammit John, we are all worried sick. What the hell are you doing?"

John just stood there, his legs wobbling.

"Oh my God, look at you!"

He was covered in white soot and blood caked in pink lumps at the corners of his mouth. Carolyn could see little trails of white where dust bypassed the mask and streamed into his nose. She made him take his clothes off in the hallway.

"John, your hands. Your hands are raw. Your whole body is black and blue. You're going to kill yourself. I can't believe you're doing this."

She led him to the shower, a naked man physically broken, but soaring in spirit.

"Carolyn, we saved a man, dug him out of the pile with our hands."

She looked at him with a face that betrayed both awe and disgust.

"I was there, at the head of the line when we found him."

Carolyn adjusted the water.

"There was just enough air for him to breathe. We saved him. We saved the man's life!"

Carolyn took off her clothes and joined her husband in the shower. It stung when the water hit his cuts and he winced when she rubbed the washcloth over his face. Carolyn lathered and scrubbed every inch of him as thick, dirty water bubbled down the drain.

Carolyn collapsed onto her husband and he could barely keep them both on their feet. Two days of the worst anguish she had ever known welled out and she sobbed in spasms as awful as John's coughs.

"Promise me you'll be safe," Carolyn wailed. "Promise me nothing will ever happen to you."

"Honey, don't worry. I promise nothing will ever happen to either of us. I'll be okay. Everyone will be okay. I've never felt so alive."

The next morning, John's eyes opened like a bolt of lightning had flashed. It wasn't even light out yet. While Carolyn was still in the bathroom the night before, he carefully laid out his clothes in a pile hidden in the hall closet. He tiptoed out of the bedroom and changed in the kitchen. He was out the door and on his bike before she woke to find him gone.

CHAPTER 61

PROFILES IN COURAGE

Parks across the town were looking better than they had in years. Bathrooms were renovated and new playgrounds went up. Fencing and sprinklers got fixed and grass grew. We put in parking lots and ball fields, replaced bulbs and flags, stopped leaks, and painted. Marinas were rebuilt and road runoff was contained, keeping it from polluting the bays. We bought a new sweeper and cleaned the parking lots. One Mayor was thrilled when we got an old mop off the roof of a bathroom that was up there for months. We even made the summer staff happy by replacing the oven-like guard booths picked out by Heart Attack that were originally built as snow huts for ski lodges. While I gained many supporters for resuscitating the parks system, I made enemies of everyone I threw off the gravy train. They weren't going away quietly. One was Heart Attack's boss, the fellow who kissed me on the cheek at the fundraiser, who was making it a career to goal to collect on a $3,000 invoice for overseeing the work at the leaky pool.

There was a red "Bat Phone" on my desk and only the Supervisor knew the number. When it rang I could be sure it was him. I was summoned to town hall and waiting for me was Heart Attack's boss—the principal of a well-heeled firm, long-time consultant to the town, generous contributor—who was aghast over the fact he wasn't getting his way. His firm did work for municipalities across Long Island and was a durable part of the local political fabric. The consultants took in loads of taxpayer dollars and dribbled pennies of it back out to a network of politicians and operatives to keep the wheels turning.

"Surely there's a way to sign off on the invoice," he asked.

I described the problems at the pool, the leaky pipes, the cracked concrete. His face reddened and the Supervisor looked on stoically as I enflamed his contributor.

"We're still out there trying to fix everything."

"It's only $3,000. What's the big deal?"

"Once we get the pool up and running, I'll get back to you," I answered, trying to find a way out.

"This is unheard of," he retorted. "We did the work, we should get paid."

I took a deep breath and was ready to launch into what I really thought. It wasn't going to be pretty.

The Supervisor cut me off. "Okay. We'll see what we can do."

To his credit, I never heard back from either of them on the subject.

A system had evolved where people lived high off the hog for very little effort and I was bucking it. It would have been easy to just sign off on the $3,000, it wasn't my money, and keep paying for shoddy work, weeds and nozzles. Live and let live was a safe motto for most everyone around me and they went along to hang onto their jobs and not get killed. But that wasn't me. I was making enemies and they were closing in, jabbing, cackling, criticizing. Each time I ruffled the system, there was a call to the Supervisor, a beef to a rabbi, or a coffee klatch of malcontents. I was heading down a dangerous path.

My Dad suggested President Kennedy's book, "Profiles in Courage," and I found an audio version recited by none other than John John himself. He describes acts of bravery and integrity by U.S. senators throughout history. The president-to-be wrote the book while recovering from back surgery for the injuries he suffered when his PT boat was sunk. It won him a Pulitzer Prize and put him on the road to the White House. These senators crossed party lines and defied popular opinion to do what they thought was right and suffered the consequences. Every year the

Kennedy family issues a Profiles in Courage Award with a trophy featuring a lantern, symbolizing the one carried by Diogenes, the ancient philosopher who searched for an honest man. John said the award was meant to help make politics a "noble and honorable profession." In local government where I resided, I could only wish it was so.

Aside from the president's "Ask not what your county can do for you..." and the lessons from Profiles in Courage, there was a comment John once made that stuck in my mind. When asked what he would do if he was ever elected, he said he would try to cut taxes. From my work as a reporter, my years with the federal government, and from where I sat as commissioner, I knew one thing for sure: The people are paying far too much for "government" and those who get the money will do just about anything to keep it coming. There's a world of difference between self-preservation and trying to change the system; between moving up the ladder or getting knocked off. I always felt John would have done what I did—try to cut through the crap and do what's right. I would have loved to have seen him in the trenches.

CHAPTER 62

THEY WILL HEAR FROM US

Back on the pile, John wrapped his fingers in white gauze and pushed them gingerly into tight gloves. His aching feet felt okay cushioned with two pairs of socks in decent boots. He adjusted his police department cap and headed to the rescue line.

"I hear the president's coming today," one of the workers said.

"I hope he kicks the shit out of whoever did this," another answered.

"Fucking terrorists. I hope Bush sticks it right up their ass."

John felt the same. A blind need for revenge burned inside of him and with each agonizing bucket he passed to the man below, his rage grew.

The man with the bullhorn spoke: "Someone very special has come here today. Please, everyone, please stop what you're doing for just a minute and give a welcome to the president of the United States. President George Bush."

The president emerged from a group of officious-looking men who were distinguished from most everyone else by not being covered in white filth. He approached a demolished fire engine that had been cleared of debris by the workers, including a man named Bob Beckwith who was asked by members of Bush's team to help the president climb onto the truck. Beckwith was retired from the New York City Fire Department and had come to the scene to help. The president kept hold of his arm and pulled him up with him. As he did, he recognized the Senator.

"Come on," the president insisted. "You're coming up here with us."

Bush took the bullhorn. "Thank you all," he said with John and the fireman at either side. "I want you all to know that America today, America today is on bended knee, in prayer for the people whose lives were lost here, for the workers who work here, for the families who mourn. The nation stands with the good people of New York City and New Jersey and Connecticut as we mourn the loss of thousands of our citizens."

A voice from the pile yelled, "I can't hear you."

The president responded, "I can hear you! I can hear you!" and the crowd let loose a cheer.

"The rest of the world hears you! And the people who knocked these buildings down will hear all of us soon!"

The crowd went wild and started chanting, "USA, USA, USA!"

Turning to John, the president continued, "I want to introduce the man who is standing with me here today, someone I understand has been at this site, working alongside everyone here. I appreciate his efforts and his patriotism for his country. Senator John Kennedy."

The crowd erupted again and kept cheering until John took the bullhorn and silenced them.

"I stand here proudly with each and every one of you," the Senator said to a crowd with heads cocked to take in his every word. "I stand here with President Bush and the United States of America."

The workers at the pile exploded and keep at it until he quieted them with a wave of his hand.

"The people who are responsible, the people who did this, they will hear from us alright. They will hear from America."

With that he gave the horn back to the president who was unable to speak through the chants of "USA, USA, USA."

It was up to John to quiet them and then President Bush concluded: "The nation sends its love and compassion to everybody who is here. Thank you for your hard work. Thank you for making the nation proud, and may God bless America."

The people of the United States, in their time of terrible tragedy and loss, were ecstatic. The president, backed by the wildly popular John F. Kennedy, Jr., had promised revenge.

James Balfour, a writer with the New York Times, filed this story:

New York, NY—We have learned the identity of the white-dusted hero pulling a fellow victim from a hellish scene at the collapsed World Trade Center and it's a shocker. From a photograph that epitomizes the brutality of the terrorist attack and mankind's innate perseverance to live emerges John F. Kennedy, Jr., U.S. Senator from New York, scion of the tragic family Camelot whose courage on the fateful day of 9/11 inspires the world.

Yet he maintains he's no hero, even as the photographic proof confirms his sturdy arm around Cantor-Fitzgerald trader Morton Kornbluth, holding the man up and guiding him to rescue.

"The fact is, Morton Kornbluth saved me," Senator Kennedy said in an exclusive interview with the New York Times. "I was knocked out when the South Tower fell, landing miraculously between two cars, and would have died there if it wasn't for Mr. Kornbluth."

According to the Senator, Kornbluth snapped him to consciousness and pulled him from the place where he was surely to perish. The older man braced his arm under the Senator's and carried him as long as he could before he, himself, collapsed. It was enough time for Kennedy to regain a modicum of strength, enough to convey both of them the rest of the way to safety.

"I don't remember very much of that day," Kornbluth said from his bed at New York Downtown Hospital. "I know that John Kennedy carried me out, but that memory may have come from just looking at the picture."

And what a picture. The iconic photograph, sure to win a Pulitzer for Associated Press Photographer Myles Pitard, shows both men sandblasted white, their black business suits tattered, emerging from a dark cloud of smoke, the rubble of immense devastation all around them. Kornbluth's leg drags at an awkward angle, a stain of blood bright red as it soaks the white powder covering his thigh. Kennedy's hair is blown black and a visage of great exertion is etched across his face as he carries the man who he swears, saved him only seconds before.

Minutes after the two made it to the ambulances, the second tower fell. They were now far enough away from the impact zone, a distance traversed under the power of Senator Kennedy, to be spared. The spot where they first came in contact, between two parked cars where Morton Kornbluth roused a stranger and then had that stranger, the esteemed senator, John F. Kennedy, Jr., take him to safety, was buried many feet deep from the remains of the great tower.

To the shock of his doctors given his battered condition, Kennedy fled the hospital September 12 and returned to Ground Zero where he worked his hands raw as a rescuer on the pile of smoldering concrete and steel that entombed thousands of innocents. Miraculously, some survived the collapse of buildings that towered 110 stories high and were pulled out, alive. Amid the burning hell, acrid smoke and dust searing his lungs, was Senator Kennedy, a hero like his father in the Pacific, digging out people and setting them free.

Kennedy was recognized as a hero on the pile when President George Bush appeared to reassure the nation after terrorists commandeered airliners to attack not only the heart of America's financial center, but the Pentagon and perhaps even the White House in a plane that was brought down in a field in southwest Pennsylvania by passengers fighting back.

"I want to introduce the man who is standing with me here today, someone I understand has been at this site, working alongside everyone here," the president said to a cheering crowd. "I appreciate his efforts and his patriotism for his country."

Chanting "USA, USA, USA," the crowd would have carried on all day if Kennedy didn't stop them. Speaking through a bullhorn passed to him by the president, the Senator stated: "I stand here proudly with each and every one of you. I stand here with President Bush and the United States of America."

Again, the workers cheered wildly and Kennedy silenced them with a wave of his hand.

"The people who are responsible," he told them, "the people who did this, they will hear from us alright. They will hear from America."

Senator Kennedy was banished from the pile by the New York City Fire Department and returned to the downtown hospital where he spent nine days recovering from his injuries.

CHAPTER 63

QUEEN OF THE ROADS

Life-altering phone calls usually come when least expected and this time, it was Supervisor LaValle again on the line.

The man who set the wheels in motion for the ascension of Mugsy was retiring and the path was clear for the first woman highway superintendent in town history. Pat Strebel was the owner of a dry cleaning store in Center Moriches and had worked on my staff in the town's Public Information Office. I don't know how she lined up the tea leaves, but when Mugsy left the town board to become kingmaker, they replaced him with Strebel. And when the highway job opened up, she got that as well, calling herself, "Queen of the Roads."

As with Henrietta and the town board, and many other candidates over the years, I worked on the Queen's campaigns. We staged photo ops with parents who were overjoyed when she put in sidewalks where kids had to walk along the side of the road to get to school. I posed her with men patching potholes and fixing drains. I even did a piece with her riding shotgun in a snowplow during a blizzard. For Christmas, she got me a desk lamp.

Trouble was right around the corner. Along the path where the new sidewalks went in were trees and roots and removing them was not part of the contract the Queen had with her vendor. So instead of 500 feet of sidewalk, the town taxpayers paid for 525, the additional monies approved by the Queen to remove the trees. Now this in itself wasn't that big of a deal—highway superintendents probably did it since they invented the automobile—but when investigators showed up with a tape measure and found 500 feet of sidewalk where the invoice read 525 and then found that the contractor and his wife and his secretary and his workers donated generously to the Queen's election, that's when it all hit the fan. The district attorney indicted her on 76 felony counts and it was a somber day at Republican headquarters when they called an emergency meeting to decide what to do.

With Mugsy out, the chairmanship was assumed by a wily old veteran who, instead of making the decision himself, went around the room and asked each of the 30 assembled zone leaders, committee members, and other political honchos, including myself, what they thought. The consensus: "We all love the Queen and it's terrible what she is going through, but there is no way we can run her for reelection."

The nomination went to Lou Gallo, a former Democrat and retired school teacher who came over to the Republican side a few years before and worked his butt off for this very moment. Nominating petitions were printed and Gallo was to run for highway superintendent on the GOP ticket with Supervisor John Jay LaValle.

"Bob, I don't want Lou Gallo," the Supervisor told me on the phone. "How would you like to run for highway superintendent?"

Opportunities like this come only once in a lifetime and I jumped at the chance. After months of swinging away in the trenches of the parks department, I was thrilled that the Supervisor recognized my work and still counted me as an asset. He said he would pull the plug on Gallo and deliver the Conservatives and the Independence Party, giving me three ballot lines that would make me hard to beat.

The Queen of the Roads would have none of it and promptly announced she would run a primary election against me for the Republican line. This divided the party and many came out against me out of deference to the Queen, who they felt was getting screwed. For those I threw off the gravy train, it was payback time and they worked harder against me than they ever did for the town. People like Heart Attack and his boss wrung their hands.

The Supervisor went right for the Queen's jugular with brochures featuring a mug shot of her behind prison bars.

"Why vote for someone with 76 corruption charges?" the campaign literature asked.

The Queen played the victim card and portrayed the race as an attack on an innocent woman. She pleaded her case to the voters in a letter printed on pink paper. I countered with my record of improving the park system and completing major projects at great savings to the taxpayers. Plus, I didn't have 76 counts hanging over my head.

On election night with my wife and supporters by my side, we watched the results come in. The Queen beat me by 680 votes and took my place on the ballot as the Republican. To her great chagrin, I remained on the Conservative and Independence lines since the only way to get off was to become a judge, move out of state or die, and I wasn't going to do any of those. Despite my not campaigning one bit because I knew I couldn't win without the GOP line, the Queen turned the seat over to the Democrats after generations of Republican control. She lost by 7,800 votes, the exact number I received on my two lines.

In a bizarre twist where you could say I got the last laugh, I was subpoenaed to testify in the Queen's trial. It was her sidewalk contractor, now her co-defendant, who did the leaky work at the Cedar Beach tower and I wouldn't sign off on his invoice. The Queen was livid.

"Were you pressured by the highway superintendent to pay this bill," the prosecutor asked.

"Yes I was."

"Can you describe the conversation?"

"She would call me on the phone and tell me to pay him."

"More than once?" the prosecutor bore in.

"Yes, on three separate occasions. What struck me the most was how nasty she was about it. She demanded that I pay him and wanted to know, 'Who the hell do you think you are?'"

"How did you respond?"

"I told her I was the commissioner and there was no way I was going to sign off on such shoddy work."

The Queen was found guilty and let off with a slap on the wrist. Her political career was over.

CHAPTER 64

OPRAH PART II

Orprah Winfrey took great pleasure in having John back on her show and wasn't about to make the embarrassing mistake she made during his last visit.

"John, I babbled like a school girl the last time you were here," she told her esteemed guest when the applause finally died down. "This time, I'm going to button my lip and let you do all the talking."

With that, the talk show titan flicked her lips with a buttoning motion and stared at the Senator with a coy smile. The audience chuckled and John sat there, a scant look of terror on his face. Oprah didn't flinch.

"Well, I guess I'm up," he smiled back at her. "Though it was a little bit easier when you did all the talking."

The audience guffawed and Oprah almost did too, a smile stretching across her pursed lips.

"Okay, I'm John F. Kennedy, Jr., Senator from New York, and I'd like to thank Oprah, my wonderful host, for having me back on her show."

He looked at her for relief, but she just grinned back at him.

"I was elected last year to succeed Senator Daniel Patrick Moynihan who was a legend in Washington serving our great state for more than 25 years. I know I won't be able to fill his shoes, but I'll give it my best."

His eyes appealed to Oprah one more time and she stayed silent, beaming at him instead.

"As a senator I am following in the footsteps of another great man, someone who I admire very much, though I didn't get to spend much time with him. My father, John Fitzgerald Kennedy, went from being senator from Massachusetts to president of the United States. At age 46, he was taken away from us and not a day goes by when I don't think of him and wonder how our world would be if he was still here."

A wave of emotion came over the studio that would be felt in the millions of homes watching the show all over the world. More than one member of the audience wiped a tear.

Now it was John who sat motionless casting his handsome gaze on a fidgeting Oprah. The audience felt the challenge. John remained quiet, frozen in time, and would say nothing more. The next words, he knew, would have to come from the host.

The audience cackled and Oprah squirmed. "I can't take it anymore," she finally gave in.

"You're following in your father's footsteps?" Oprah asked breathlessly. "He was a senator and now you're a senator. He became president. John, are you telling us you are running for president?"

It was John's turn to clam up and he mimicked Oprah in buttoning his lip. Warm smiles spread across their faces and the audience roared.

"I guess he's giving me a taste of my own medicine," she said as she stared at him back.

"Truce!" John called out. "And I must say, this is a whole lot easier when you're asking the questions."

"Okay, okay, I'll ask the questions. John," Oprah said slapping her hands on her knees. "Will you be our president?"

The audience went crazy again and the show cut to a commercial break.

No one in the next four minutes changed the channel and the money spent by Oprah's advertisers in that time block surely got a tremendous bang for their buck.

After the break Oprah did the talking.

"We are back with Senator John Kennedy who has ratcheted up the suspense by mentioning the word 'president.' I have asked him flat out if he will be running for the White House, but before I put the pressure on him, we've prepared some clips to share some of his life and the tragedies and triumphs this great man has experienced. Please, watch."

The studio lit up with images of a mischievous tyke hiding under an enormous desk, his dad, the president of the United States, beaming with delight. He gets a hug from his father, a loving embrace that washes a sigh through the Oprah audience.

Next is the solemn procession heading down Pennsylvania Avenue with mourners lining the streets and then the little boy saluting his fallen dad. John is pictured growing up, his moppish hair giving way to a close cut emphasizing his chiseled features. His Olympian body emerges from the sea and the audience squeals. Here he is with his mom, the enigmatic Jackie O, and hugging his sister Caroline and then coming out to the world at the Democratic national convention. At work now, he's at the editor's desk, covers of his magazine zipping by with Cindy Crawford as George Washington, Drew Barrymore as Marilyn Monroe, Gisele Bündchen in an American flag bikini, Kate Moss, naked, in the Garden of Eden, and Demi Moore in a billowing red and white striped dress cracked open to show the Father of Our Country at the end of puppet strings. The audience guffaws and then a picture of John flashes with his arm held high in victory on election night. They cheer and are quickly silenced by the picture of John at Ground Zero, his face showing the strain of carrying the man he saved.

"An extraordinary life, Mr. Senator," Oprah speaks up as the last image fades. The audience launches a standing ovation which Oprah tries to stop but cannot. John looks at her and smiles. He then overemphasizes a wave of his hand and the crowd drops dead silent. Then they all laugh.

"Okay, tell us if that screen will be showing you in the White House someday," Oprah asked point blank.

"We'll see."

"Come on John, everyone wants to know. Will you be president of the United States?"

"I'll tell you what, when I make up my mind, I'll make sure you and your audience are the first to know."

Oprah knew she should give it a rest.

"Tell us what it's like to be in Washington following in your family's footsteps."

"Well there's one thing that I always keep in the back of my mind and it's something I know my dad was very passionate about and that is giving everybody an opportunity to succeed, to make sure everyone has a fair chance at the American dream."

"How's the nation coming along on that front," the host asked.

"Okay, but there's still a lot of work to be done. There is still poverty and in too many areas, the educational opportunities are less than in others."

"What are you going to do about it?"

"I can tell you one thing, the answer is not more government. As I've said, I wanted as much real world experience I could get before jumping into politics and as a businessman I know that inspiration and innovation springs from the people, not the government."

"Go on."

"As a senator, I am forever lobbied by people associated with the system, the people who make their living from it. So I make it a point to meet with the other side, the average citizens, the working families who pay the bills. And you know what? They all tell the same story. Oprah, the system isn't working for them. Paying for all this government is a huge burden and it's the one thing, I think, that's holding the country back."

"What's the answer?"

"The simplest and easiest thing we can do?" he looked at his host with his dead serious gaze. "Cut taxes. Let the people keep their money. Trust me, they know what to do with it and I guarantee they can ensure the nation's prosperity a lot better than the politicians."

"What about a helping hand?" Oprah asked. "What about the people who need the government to help them?"

"That's been going on for a half a century, longer, and yet, not much has changed. You want to see a real renaissance in this country, make it more affordable to live here by getting government off the people's back."

The audience erupted and their applause drowned out the host as she closed out the show.

CHAPTER 65

THE CAT

During the heyday of the Republican Party in Suffolk County, a place where President Ronald Regan beat Walter Mondale by 100,000 votes, a political insider named James Catterson announced he was running to replace the retiring district attorney. He called on people to support him with a simple message: If you're not on board and I win, you will be on the bad side of a very powerful man. If you said yes, you were okay and in short order, the Republican lined up all the support he'd need. The Democrats, wise to their own self-preservation, played a game of their own: To the outside world, they were behind their candidate, but in reality, they weren't going to do anything to upset The Cat.

I was president of the Brookhaven Town Young Republican Club at the time and represented a political work force of about 100 go-getters. I invited The Cat to a meeting where I announced the club's liaisons to each of the upcoming political campaigns. I assigned YR's to the supervisor's race, town clerk, council, legislators and when I got to the office of the district attorney, The Cat, as if we had timed it, came through the door. He was an older man, balding and I introduced him to two young attorneys who would be working his race. Doubling down, I also assigned myself. He was delighted and I was proud of my shrewd move of connecting our club so directly to the soon-to-be DA. Before the week was through, I edited his bio and wrote his first press release. His background as a Korean War vet, prosecutor, legislative counsel and government insider was impressive and his political reach was underscored by the million dollar fee he had collected from Nassau County for trying to stop the landing of the Concord supersonic jet at John F. Kennedy Airport.

As in most elections where the fix is in, The Cat's challenger was pretty much on his own, though inexplicably, it was The Cat himself who gave him his biggest boost. It's an incident I use to drive home the point that a candidate—or anyone speaking publicly for that matter—needs to go in with talking points and stick to the script, never answering questions off the top of their head and risk revealing their true identity. The Cat didn't think this rule applied to him and during a News 12 television debate, in response to a question about domestic violence, uttered, "I'm not going to prosecute every man who belts his wife across the face." By the next morning, his opponent rallied the women's groups who called on The Cat to drop out of the race. The bad press made the vote a lot closer than it would have been.

With The Cat in charge, political business went on as usual since everyone working the system supported him and he spent his time getting headlines at the expense of drug dealers, crooks and creeps. When the Democrats floated a rumor that the Monarch was running a numbers racket, The Cat told him he had nothing to worry about. And when Mugsy went down, it wasn't at the hands of the Suffolk DA, but the FBI, leaving many to wonder what The Cat knew about Mugsy and when did he know it. Maybe if he dished out some tough love to the up and comers, Mugsy and the Monarch wouldn't have gotten themselves into so much trouble.

The Cat's opponent for the next election was a sacrificial lamb by the milquetoast name of Tad Scharfenburg. Despite some bad press for driving around in a late-model BMW he confiscated from a drug dealer, The Cat was swept back in. There were some, however, who wandered off the reservation and five Democrats working for the Town of Babylon would find out what it meant to be on his bad side. The Cat charged the Babylon Five with illegally transferring money between different accounts to make the books look better than they really were. Those in the know rolled their eyes at such a blatant political hit and the case fell apart at trial with four getting off scot-free and a slap on the wrist for the fifth.

The Cat went on undeterred and tangled with anyone who got in his way, though no one could have guessed that the events leading to his demise would be set in motion not by the politicians he feuded with, but by a little girl.

Two days shy of her tenth birthday, Katie Beers was lured by the promise of presents to the home of a family friend who kidnapped and imprisoned her in a six-by-seven-foot underground bunker concealed by a 200-pound trap door made of concrete. Along with other children in the neighborhood, Katie had played in the dirt displaced by the dungeon as her captor dug it. The family friend was a suspect from the start and after 16 days, led police to the child he had trapped.

Katie's story was national news and Jim Catterson was at the microphone for almost all of the coverage. Also jostling for the limelight was another local law enforcement honcho, Sheriff Patrick Mahoney, who sent out a press release saying the little girl was safe and sound in the foster care of one of his deputies. The DA was livid and Mahoney said The Cat threatened to arrest him if he didn't butt out of the case. The bad blood between the Irishmen recast the definition of "Political Vendetta." After appearing in court himself to prosecute the Katie Beers case, The Cat made good on his threat and busted Mahoney and his campaign manager on 90 counts for running his reelection out of the sheriff's office, with a side charge of illegally giving out special sheriff badges to his supporters. The case went to trial and sitting at the defense table was another attorney with a long pedigree in police and politics, a contemporary who was going up against The Cat in more ways than one. Tom Spota was a Republican, but announced a switch to the Democrat side to challenge The Cat for district attorney.

Sensing a changing of the guard, Catterson's detractors were emboldened and began to speak out. At the time, The Cat's son was working in the county attorney's office and drafted the contract for a car leasing deal that had come under fire by the legislature. That body's presiding officer went public saying the DA threatened to empanel a grand jury against him if he didn't back off. The county's health commissioner said The Cat bullied her after she refused to alter the psychological test results of a man he wanted to hire and the head of the department of civil service said The Cat threw him out of his building because he wanted the office space.

With the political world tuned in like it was a soap opera, Mahoney put a halt to his own trial and pleaded guilty to three misdemeanors in exchange for no jail time and a proviso that he could keep his job as sheriff. His deputy pleaded guilty to one felony and four misdemeanors. He, too, avoided jail time.

CHAPTER 66

SAME AS THE OLD BOSS

The Cat was upsetting the apple cart and it was easy for Spota to line up the coalition he would ride to victory, the last piece being the law enforcement community, typically strong advocates of the district attorney, which turned on The Cat after the Mahoney fiasco. Spota dredged up The Cat's gaffe about not prosecuting men who slap their wives and won bigger than even he expected. He promptly paid back the favor to the Democrats by going after the Republicans in Brookhaven, The Cat's home turf. His first target, the Queen of the Roads.

Spota put the town under a microscope and there was little doubt more dominoes would fall. Next went "Tony Tickets," a low-level town employee who sold Republican fundraiser tickets when he should have been working. There was Dickman, the GOP treasurer who was shaking down zoning board applicants. The new DA went after the guys in public safety for fibbing about training reports and then got the chief building inspector for receiving cash and services to fast-track construction projects. The plumbing inspector also went down and another employee was rung up for faking his time sheets. A Republican contributor, a long-time real estate broker, was busted for putting the wrong information on a building permit form. Another score was a Republican legislator who was spending campaign money on himself.

As try as he may, the Supervisor could not contain the self-servers. The long Republican reign was coming to an end and John LaValle announced he would not seek reelection.

During the thick of it, I started getting phone calls from people who said Spota's men were asking them about me. It was suggested I get a lawyer and three names were recommended, one of whom sounded familiar, so I retained him. A few days later, detectives stopped me at the post office and wanted me to come in for questioning. I had nothing to hide and gave them the name of my lawyer to set it up. As I found out later, this was like waving a red flag in front of a pack of bulls. My attorney had an interesting background which hadn't dawned on me until it was too late: when The Cat went after the Babylon Five and lost, it was my lawyer who represented them. The detectives, investigators and prosecutors who lost the case stayed on when Spota came aboard and were looking to settle the score. My tit was heading for the ringer.

The investigation dragged on for months and judging by the amount of calls I got from people who were questioned and the crap they came up with at the end, I figure the DA spent a million dollars trying to get me. They never did set up a meeting, only notifying my attorney that I would be arrested and setting a date when I had to turn myself in. For maximum effect, the detectives waltzed me through a perp walk as I went from booking to the arraignment in my special bracelets. The town board suspended me without pay the next day and my mug shot and the DA's triumph in nailing "another corrupt Brookhaven politician" was all over the press. The turd had plopped squarely on my plate.

In the days that followed, an amazing thing happened: my phone never stopped ringing and people came to my house, some who I hadn't seen in years, to wish me well and opine over how ridiculous the whole thing seemed.

Chapter 67

NEXT TIME

John was nowhere to be found when the Oprah show aired and it was a good thing: the Four Men and much of Democrat establishment were mortified. John's words about cutting taxes and getting government off the backs of the people were like daggers to their heart. In one fell swoop, their hero erased a lifetime of Liberal philosophy and put the Republican theory of trickledown economics back on the front burner.

Bill and Hillary were ecstatic. "Honey, we're back in the race," the ex-president gleefully announced to the former first lady. "John's name is officially mud with the left wing and we're going to leap frog right over him. We're heading back to the Oval Office!"

They did a little jig together in the middle of the room.

The Four Men were not so sure and huddled in an opulent Harlem apartment to think things through.

"He's the only one who can beat Bush," the first one said.

"I'm not so sure," said the second. "He's pissed off a lot of Democrats."

"He's gotta get through the Clintons first," countered the third. "I'm sure they already have the wheels in motion."

"They do," interjected the fourth. "Secretary of State is off the table. They're already telling people they're going hard." He looked around the table to see his colleagues in deep thought.

"Who's it gonna be, gentleman?"

"Kennedy. He may have fucked up, but he's unbeatable."

"Clinton. We need someone who gets it, someone who sees things our way."

"That's fine and dandy if you want to back a loser," the banter went around again to the first. "If Bush gets back in, we're all losers. With a heavy heart, I'm with John."

"So it's down to me," said the fourth. His three colleagues spoke at once and he rose to his feet, waiving them off.

"Our whole lives we've been engaged in this struggle, fighting for the same decency provided to everyone else in this country. We stood with Martin Luther and watched him die. We cast our lot with Bobbie only to see him go. The Clintons? They were okay and we did pretty well for ourselves, but not as good as we should have. Now we have a dilemma on our hands and we need to make a decision. What's the best move? Who's got the best shot at winning this thing?"

He rubbed his chin.

"I saw those crowds in Harlem. Jesus himself couldn't have done better. The man was at the pile and he dug people out with his bare hands. His picture coming out of the ashes like some kind of savior is the most riveting of the century. For Christ's sake, if this kid wants to be the president of the United States, I say we let him."

The next stop for the Four Men was a meeting with the Senator himself and they bought with them a small, wiry man who talked a mile a minute.

"John, this is Phil Goldstone, the premier electoral consultant in the country." John nodded.

"He's played a pivotal role in the last..."

Goldstone didn't let him finish.

"We need to build a team in Iowa and crank it up in New Hampshire. Get momentum here and Super Tuesday's ours. We can't blow Super Tuesday. And don't forget Florida," he said without stopping for a breath. "Ignore Florida and get trounced. We win Florida and the Clintons have no chance. What about the Clintons?" he shot a glance at the Four Men. "What's the story on the Clintons? Are they in or are they out? What about secretary of state? Did anyone hear from Gore? I gotta know what Gore's up to."

"Gentlemen. Please." John waived his hand. "I thank you very much for your support and I really appreciate your coming to see me. I've been in office only a year and a half and jumping into the presidential race is just not something I'm thinking about right now."

"But Senator," the fourth spoke up, "with all due respect, it's your destiny."

"Agreed, but not right now."

"It's your only chance," another of the Four said, "with all due respect."

Goldstone deflated into a chair.

"With all due respect back to you, I don't think it's my only chance."

"Will you support the Democrat?" the largest of the four asked, surprising even himself with his pushiness.

John stared at him for a moment, his eyes taking on a demeanor the big man knew all too well. "We'll jump off that bridge when we get to it, okay?"

Back out on Third Avenue, the consultant excused himself and bee-lined it to the nearest bar. The Four Men were crushed.

"Son of a bitch," said The First. "So much for that game plan."

Senator Kennedy laid low for most of the Democrat primary which came down to Hillary and the Senator from Massachusetts, John Kerry. Cursing Kennedy, the Four Men threw their weight behind Clinton who was poised to make history as the nation's first woman president. Goldstone left the reservation and went to work for Kerry, his expertise winning the Iowa Caucuses and then the New Hampshire primary. The Clinton's went into panic mode.

"We have to make the deal," Hillary told Bill. "If I lose, we have nothing. If we drop out now, I'll take secretary of state."

"Are you sure?" Bill replied. "You won't be satisfied with that. You want to be president. This is about you being the president."

"But if I lose I won't be anything."

Bill gave his wife a hug. "You'll still have me."

"A lot of good that will do."

Clinton made her deal and dropped out of the race. Kerry and Bush went at it like gladiators. The former Texas governor, who entered office with a robust domestic agenda modeled after successes in his home state, had been thrown into the role of War President in his first year. His approval rating soared from his focus on revenge after 9/11 and his invasion of Afghanistan and Iraq riveted the nation. Osama Bin Laden and Saddam Hussein, not John Kerry, were his biggest foes. But the drudge of war soured the nation and attacks by the Democrats over the absence of weapons of mass destruction—Bush's primary reason for invading Iraq— weakened the president. The public began to turn on George Bush number two.

Kerry himself was a war veteran having served in Viet Nam and spoke with authority on military issues. That is until he was "Swift Boated." A group of veterans who had served with Kerry on the boats used to rapidly penetrate enemy defenses called into question his anti-war statements following Viet Nam and painted him as a hypocrite.

The Four Men appealed to Senator Kennedy.

"Our man's sinking fast and there's only one person who can save him," they told John who, up to that time, had stayed out of the presidential sweepstakes.

"The race for president is not about me," he told his suitors.

"But your endorsement would mean the difference in the race."

John had contemplated the very scenario and had his answer ready.

"This is John Kerry's race to win or lose. I've raised millions for the cause and the rest is up to him. I think he should sink or swim in his own right."

The Four Men were flabbergasted.

"You have the ability to change history," the fourth came back. "Your words will mean the difference between four more years of George Bush or a Democrat back in the White House."

"I'm sorry, gentlemen, I just don't want to play that role."

The Four Men were back on the street madder than hornets.

"Goddamn him," one of them said. "Has too much of a mind of his own. Not a team player."

"We give him every chance in the book, serve it up to him like a softball, and he tells us to go to hell every time," said another. "Screw him."

"Gentlemen, please, you know what this is about," the fourth settled them down. "If Kerry wins he'll be up for reelection in four years and Kennedy will have a hard case to run against a fellow Democrat."

The men shook their heads knowingly.

"If Bush gets back in, it'll be John's after that."

"Man knows how to play his cards."

"Amen to that."

CHAPTER 68

SAND BAGGED

Here's what the district attorney had on me: When I took my tour of all the park facilities I visited a set of baseball fields the town leased to a youth group for a dollar a year. There was some machinery at the site and it looked like they were building more fields. I asked for a meeting with the group leaders to see what was going on and they showed me plans for three new diamonds, which I thought were wonderful. Anything I could do to shift the town's priorities toward actually doing something good for the public I did. To help them out, I put in requisitions for landscape shrubs and clay for the infields. I also referred the matter to the town planning board and they approved the new fields as a "miscellaneous item."

At this point, let me say from almost the day I started, I had regular meetings with a team from an internationally-known investigation firm hired by Supervisor LaValle to make sure everything in the town was on the up and up. They scoured the department's files, including my feet of paperwork every week, and we discussed everything that was going on. Though the scrutiny added to my work load, I welcomed it to make sure everything was clean.

With the mountain of issues confronting me in changing the parks department from the ground up, a youth league building ball fields was the least of my worries and I didn't give the matter much thought until I was invited to throw out the first ball on opening day. I brought along my Dad and we were introduced to a young lady who won an essay contest for the chance to catch the first pitch. With dozens of kids and parents looking on, the commissioner took the mound and tossed a slow lob to the girl, who created a nice target with her mitt directly in front of her face. Just before the ball arrived, she moved the mitt to check its progress and got hit right on the forehead. Down she went as a collective gasp rose from the crowd. Then she popped back up rubbing her head none the worse for the wear and the crowd cheered. I sauntered off amongst the chaos and beat it to the next event.

Even though I almost knocked off one of their players, the youth leaders appreciated my support and when I ran for highway superintendent, they sent out a letter urging the parents of the kids to vote for me. According to the DA, however, when the league built the new fields, they took sand from the property, sand which they bartered for top soil, fencing and other materials. This was 12 months before I ran for office. By the district attorney's reckoning, I committed a crime for supposedly letting them take the sand in exchange for a letter of support in an election that would occur a year later. I was flabbergasted and anyone who knew me or had any familiarity with local government knew it was a political hit, pure and simple. The DA wanted to show he was "cleaning out" corruption in Brookhaven and bagging a commissioner was a home run. I wasn't charged with bribery or stealing or anything else that sounded like a crime. I was charged with "official misconduct in the second degree"—the DA and his henchmen spent a ton of taxpayer money, abused the power of their office to settle some egomaniacal score with my lawyer and charged me with two felony counts because they didn't like *my* conduct.

Chapter 69

HEADLINES

The National Enquirer had a field day with their favorite target:

"John John Caught in Office Tryst With Staffer."

"Carolyn Won't Fly With John, Calls Him 'Reckless.'"

"Kennedy Junkets in Puerto Rico While Carolyn Pouts at Home."

"Senator Kennedy Banished by the Democrats."

"Ted Kennedy Plots Against His 'Wild' Senator Nephew."

"John Rekindles Flame With Daryl."

"Senator Haunted by Ground Zero Ghosts."

"Is Madonna Stalking John John?"

"Carolyn Hides Baby Bump."

"Oh my God," Sandra blurted out at the bar. "They're going to have a baby?" She looked at me with admiring eyes. "You big softy. I didn't think you had it in you."

It was true. Carolyn was pregnant and their favorite tabloid was beside itself.

"Carolyn Reluctant to Bring Another Kennedy Into the World."

"John Devastated: It's Not Going to be a Boy."

And then the capper even for Enquirer standards: "Friends Fear It's Not His."

John, who maintained his Secret Service moniker from when he was a boy in the White House, "Lark," was asked to meet with the director of the federal agency that protects politicians and presidents.

"Senator, there's been an uptick in chatter about plots against you," the director told him. "Outside of the jealous husbands and the Tea Party nuts, we're getting more serious stuff. Maybe even al Qaeda."

John took on a concerned expression and nodded.

"We're going to step up your security and ask that you make your schedule a little less public."

"No way you bastard. Don't you touch a hair on his head," Sandra was pissed.

"What are you talking about?" I grinned.

"I know what you're doing. You're setting up his assassination. If you kill him I'll never forgive you."

"Okay, okay, relax. I'm not going to assassinate John John."

"You better not. He's going to be the next president and live happily ever after and so is John F. Kennedy the Third."

"Who says it's going to be a boy?"

"He's going to be a boy. Got it?

"Got it."

Chapter 70

PILING ON

After the DA busted me, the Democrats piled on like I was Boss Tweed. With every press release from the prosecutor came a slew of pot shots at me in the papers. The biggest mouth was Brian Foley, a lifelong political hack who started working as an aide for his father right out of college and when he retired, inherited his seat in the county legislature. Brian now had his sights set on town supervisor and promised to "Clean up Crookhaven."

A month before Election Day, the DA had yet to drop his bomb on me and I was still the commissioner. Foley scheduled a press conference to bemoan his belief that Neville Park, a waterfront area in my hometown of Center Moriches, was being ignored by the evil Republicans. The only problem was we had just nailed down the state permits needed to renovate the park and men and machinery were already on the scene. I told them to lay low and when I gave the signal, the nose flick Robert Redford used in *The Sting*, they were to fire up all their equipment—generators, excavators, pumps—and get to work. Foley attracted a pretty good crowd and the second he opened his mouth, I flicked my nose. He had to yell above the din to read his script and the reporters looked at him like he was an idiot. When he was done, I rolled out the blueprints and went over the new bulkheading, walkways, and other improvements we were making to the park. He accused me of sabotaging his press conference. I accused him of being a moron.

The Suffolk County Democrats used their offices like hiring halls to lard up the public payroll with people to work on their elections and kick back campaign money. The hirings cost millions and soon, their budget numbers didn't add up. They learned their lesson from High Tax Halpin and didn't dare balance the books by raising taxes. They didn't want to get rid of all the hacks they hired, so they went after the weakest, the county nursing home in Yaphank. Championed by Brian's father during his years on the legislature, it was named after him, the John J. Foley Skilled Nursing Center. The Democrats tried to sell it, but instead of a public bidding process, they arranged a backroom deal with a sales price $13 million less than an offer made a year before. To make it even more lucrative for their buyer, they threw in 14 acres of vacant land surrounding the home. When you have the DA on your team you can make moves like this without worrying about being arrested for misconduct.

The workers rolled out patients in wheelchairs to protest the sale and it became one of the county's most contentious issues. The facility was located in Brookhaven and the town's zoning board shot down development plans for the 14 acres causing the deal to collapse. The county ended up closing the home, forcing out the patients and putting people out of work. Every politician took a stand on the issue except for one, the former legislator, town supervisor, and state senator Brian Foley, who couldn't be bothered.

Democrat critiques to the contrary, there was never a moment of my time as commissioner when I didn't stand up for what was right, to change the old way of doing things, to wring savings from the steady stream of business that crossed my desk and do what's right for the taxpayers. I treated the employees with respect and the Union-Management Partnership was a shining example of how you can run a department effectively in the swamp of local politics. When there once was a grievance filed by the employees almost every week, there were none during my four-year tenure and dozens of projects, now with the hand of the workforce involved at every phase, were getting done. I truly believe I made a difference.

The Internet chatter had it right:

"Saw the article this afternoon on Newsday's website about the arrest of Bob Chartuk, Parks Commissioner for the Town of Brookhaven. What a ridiculous trumped up charge! To allege that he had the town remove half a million dollars worth of sand from a Patchogue ball field in order to get a $750 contribution to his failed campaign is moronic. Anyone who knows Bob Chartuk knows that he is a kind, good and honest man. The DA should be going after the real criminals in Crookhaven, especially in the business of delivering bribe money to the building department."

And this:

"The biggest question is, or should be: WHO, IF ANYONE BENEFITTED from this? We don't know that because no one told us. All we heard is the guy gave up a lot of sand and got a $750 campaign donation in return. Don't sound like a big deal to me. I think it is far worse for a district attorney to have police officers going around collecting campaign donations for him and then have them assigned to his office after he gets elected. One eyewitness actually told me he saw one such cop don a windbreaker while he was on duty and go door to door soliciting contributions for a candidate. Maybe the sand would have been put to better use if it was taken to the courtyard outside the DA's office and dumped there so his detectives can go out each day and play in the sandbox."

And this (not sure about the priests and nuns):

"The guy gave the sand to the Little League, not the NY Yankees for season box seats. It sounds like the guy was only trying to do a good deed. No good deed goes unpunished. Doesn't sound too nefarious to me, and surely the DA office knows all about 'nefarious' people - they had a judge declare 21 such folks such, including a priest and two nuns."

CHAPTER 71

THE CHALLENGER

John scanned the floor of the United States Senate and keyed in on the one man who worried him: Barack Obama, a former state senator from Illinois who spent time in New York City studying at Columbia and was the first black editor of the Harvard Review. He started in politics as a community organizer and launched his bid for public office with a book, "Dreams from My Father: A Story of Race and Inheritance." He was a staunch opponent of Bush's war in Iraq while John voted for it. John was certain Obama wanted to be the first black president.

He got in touch with Phil Goldstone, the man who delivered the primary for Kerry.

"I'm not worried about this newcomer from Illinois," the consultant jumped right in. "Can't hold a candle to you. I still have the apparatus in Iowa and New Hampshire looks good. What about the Clintons? Is secretary of state on the table? They can't possibly go with the other guy and would be nuts to go up against you. The Republicans? They got nobody. Plus who's going to vote for them after the Bush disaster? Not for nothing, Senator, and I'm not kissing your ass, but you're like a god out there. I don't give a rat's butt about what anyone else does, you're going to be our next president."

"Thank you Phil," John shoehorned himself in. "What I'm really worried about is the black community. If Obama announces for president, I'm going to lose their support."

"What?" Goldstone retorted. "The Kennedys have done more for the blacks than Abraham Lincoln. They're not going to turn on you."

"From your lips to God's ears," the Senator replied.

CHAPTER 72

THE PROOF WASN'T IN THE PUDDING

Politics is a nasty business and the district attorney's henchmen did everything in their power to take out an up and coming Republican. Now they had to prove their case.

It cost $2,500 to retain my attorney and he wanted $250,000 more for a trial and another go at the DA boys. I knew we could beat them, but I didn't have a quarter million dollars to fight for justice. I got another lawyer and this time found one who had better relations with the DA's office (he used to work there). I had to pay him $20,000 and in retrospect, had I retained him from day one I'm sure it never would have come to this. In fact, had I not even hired an attorney and simply told the detectives that day at the post office to set up a meeting with me and the prosecutor from the Queen of the Roads case, they probably wouldn't have had a problem with my conduct at all. Better yet, I should have just become a Democrat.

With my new attorney on board, I was offered a deal: plead guilty to a misdemeanor and they would go easy on me. I told them to go scratch and said I looked forward to the trial. A date was set and that morning I put on my best suit, kissed my wife goodbye and went to the courthouse to prove my innocence. The assistant district attorney handling the case asked for a one-month postponement, but not before Spota's office sent out another press release dragging me through the mud. A month later, I put on my suit, kissed my wife and headed for my trial. Postponed again and another press release. Month three: put on my suit, kissed my wife and dragged through again. Another offer came—they would go easy on me if I wore a wire to entrap some of the people I used to work with. I told them to kiss my ass. If they think they have such a great case where they felt the need to ruin my career and badger me in the press every month, then they should get on with the trial.

The routine was designed to pressure me into providing information on leads they were working which, to my mind, were on the other side of bizarre. They were most interested in a tall tale that had parks employees taking town equipment and materials to build a dock at a councilman's father's house. If this had indeed occurred, during work hours no less, it would have been quite a cover up, but that didn't matter to the DA who was going to great lengths to take down Republicans. I guess they didn't care about the overpriced consulting, vanishing equipment and the laundry list of shoddy work I was up against. The scenarios they pursued were preposterous and it was clear that those feeding the investigators were pulling rabbits out of their hats to save their own skin.

One doozy I can trace back to a single source, a former Democrat who I thought was one of the biggest weasels in the bunch.

Because purchasing material and equipment was critical to town operations, especially for large-scale projects like the ones we did in the park departments, Supervisor LaValle asked me to take over as the town purchasing director. Soon after word of that got out, the county Department of Civil Service magically scheduled a test for the position, clearly an orchestrated effort to knock me out of the box. The job could now only go to those scoring high enough on the test to be "reached." The Weasel suggested I contact his friend who was a purchasing director in another town and could help me prepare for the exam. I met with him once and he reiterated what I already knew, that civil service exams are more like IQ tests to see if you have the *ability* to do the job, not if you know *how* to do the job.

The test was given in two locations and the room I was in was packed with more than 100 people, including a few ladies from

Brookhaven's purchasing department. The one piece of advice I read over and over in preparing for the test was to pay attention to the instructions at the beginning. The proctor told us we had eight hours to complete the exam and if we wanted to go to the bathroom there were people that had to go with us. There was no talking, make sure you fill in the circles completely, use a number two pencil, no pens, blah, blah, blah. I didn't pay much attention and just wanted to get on with it.

The test booklet was thick with questions and the first section was made up of complicated math exercises, which I was okay with. Next were purchasing scenarios that seemed alien, like they weren't providing enough information to arrive at the correct answers. I felt nauseous as I narrowed down my choices, wondering the whole time if I was missing something. The room thinned out, some giving up after only a few minutes, and I finished up thinking I was a complete failure.

Then I noticed a second booklet on the desk, one which I would have known about had I been paying attention to the proctor. It was the background information for the scenarios they were basing the questions on.

My God, I thought, The Holy Grail!

Now it was just a matter of locating the missing data and answering the questions I struggled with for most of the day. I went back and double and triple checked my card and after eight grueling hours, was the last person to leave.

A few weeks later, a letter arrived from the civil service department and I was afraid to open it. How big of a loser would I be if the Supervisor wanted me to straighten out purchasing like I did the parks department and couldn't do it because I failed the test? Hands shaking, I opened the envelope. Number three. Out of hundreds of people, many of who worked in town purchasing departments across the county, I came in number three.

Only two people knew I met with the other purchasing director, the guy himself and the Weasel who made the introduction. If I could shed some light on how the purchasing director fixed the civil service test, the DA wanted to know, they would let me off the hook in that investigation. I told them they were getting their chains yanked and if they really wanted to ferret out the crooks in government they should start with the people who were feeding them this crap. The lengths political hacks like the Weasel would go to screw someone to save their own skin shouldn't amaze me, but it still does.

CHAPTER 73

THEY'VE HAD THEIR TIME

Four somber faces greeted John at his office in the Russell Senate building. The Black Men had travelled to Washington for an "Emergency Meeting" with the Senator and they went in nervous and fidgety.

The meeting before the meeting was a torturous affair as the Four Men debated their fate.

"I'm still with Kennedy, one hundred percent," said the first. "He's more popular now than he's ever been with that new baby boy and I don't think there's anything on earth that's going to stop him."

"We're batting zero for zero with this kid," said the second, throwing his hands up in disgust. "We ask him to run for president and he blows us off. And then he says 'no' when we ask him to come out for Kerry and gives us four more years of Bush. And then he goes on TV and starts talking about tax cuts and the failure of government programs. Are we out of our minds? I say we cut our losses, go for our own guy, Barack Obama."

"We are talking about the first black president," said the third. "We may never get this chance again. The Kennedys, they've had their time. It's time for us."

"I'm going to end this right now," said the fourth. "My history goes back to the Kennedys further than any of us and God knows how I'd like John to make it. But this Obama thing, it's just too compelling. The moment we've been waiting for our whole lives is here. We just need to step up to the plate. I'm for Barack Obama. Senator Obama for president of the United States."

"It's going to be a battle Royale," the first wouldn't go down without a fight. "John's going to win and we'll be screwed."

"We will be on the right side of history."

"Fine, but what will that get us?"

"It's up to us. We have to deliver the vote. The power is in our hands, gentlemen. We can put our man in the White House."

"What if..."

"That's it," the second cut him off. "The vote is three to one. Obama is our man."

Before they could get a word out, John launched into a soliloquy he had prepared in his head.

"Gentlemen, in my relatively short time in elected office, you have been by my side and I truly appreciate all your support. You were with me at the Apollo Theater when we announced my run for the senate and even though I didn't go for president the last time around, I know you were behind me and I want you to know that means a lot to me. Well, now, the time is right. I am going to run for the presidency and I hope I can once again count on your support."

John slowly scanned his visitors. "You don't look very enthusiastic."

"We came here to give you the bad news personally, Senator," the fourth one spoke up. "We've decided to take a bow to history and go with Obama. We hope you understand."

John was hurt. He felt he could always count on the Four Men. They always supported him, supported his family.

"I understand," he said rising to his feet and extending his hand. "No hard feelings."

The first one grabbed John's hand and shook it profusely. The others surrounded them in a bear hug.

"No hard feelings."

All four of them looked down at the pavement when they got out to Constitution Avenue.

"He's going to kick our ass," said the first."

"I hope you're wrong," said the second.

"We all hope you're wrong."

CHAPTER 74

SAMURAI

My showdown with the DA was postponed six times and if you really want to take the measure of a man, arrest him, fire him, drain his bank account, put out so much bad press no one would give him a job, postpone his trial six times, and then see how he does. "What doesn't kill you makes you stronger," the saying goes, and I emerged a Hercules!

When I kissed my wife the sixth time, it wasn't at home. I had dropped her off at the hospital for shoulder surgery, kidding that I didn't know she pitched for the Yankees. Her injury is actually common with mothers who awkwardly stretch their arms to take care of the baby in the back seat. I would have liked to have been there for her, but I worked in an arena where scum bags thought it was better to play politics to prop up their own miserable careers than do what's right for people. I went to the courthouse and reemphasized the fact that I had the right to a speedy trial and wasn't leaving without a fight. They delayed it again and it took a while for my lawyer to convince me it would be in my best interests to go.

Back at the hospital, my wife was resting comfortably so I went out to the car for a break. I had six messages from my attorney telling me to come back ASAP. I hustled my wife out of post-op, dropped her off at home, and returned to the courthouse. As I pulled into the lot I saw two news trucks with satellite dishes on top and dozens of people looming around. I got my attorney on the phone and he told me not to worry, the crowd was there for a different case. In the courtroom next to mine they were arraigning a teenager for chopping off his stepfather's head while he slept, the infamous Samurai Murder Case.

My courtroom was empty and soon the prosecutor appeared with one of the detectives, each plopping a box of files on the table and looking at me like I was supposed to be intimated by all of the "evidence." It included the approval of the fields by the planning board which I had somehow coerced and a rambling statement from the youth league president who we were itching to tear apart on the stand. They even entered into evidence a picture of me throwing out the first pitch on the new fields. I stared back at the prosecutors with a look that said, "Big fucking deal."

My attorney arrived and they hustled into the back, leaving me to sit alone on a wooden bench in the gallery. I imagined how the trial would go, how the DA's witnesses would hold up under the cross examinations we had in store for them. Running for highway superintendent was the last thing I thought I would do when those fields were built and we were looking forward to seeing how the DA would make the connection. How is it possible that I gave the league permission to take sand in exchange for a letter in a campaign that would happen 12 months later?

My attorney was worried that a jury would take their disdain for politicians out on me. A bench trial with a judge would be a risk as well since he would probably be beholden to the system and would screw me. I dreamed of the moment I was declared, "Not guilty."

The door of the courtroom opened and the district attorney himself came in. I stood up.

"Hello Mr. Spota."

"Hello Bob."

"Keep up the good work," I told him as I shook his hand.

"You too." he replied and disappeared into the back.

I ducked outside to see what was going on with the samurai case. The door was guarded by two court officers and the room was packed. Camera crews were set up in the corridor and the dozens of people who couldn't get in were buzzing around.

Thank God they're not all here for me, I thought to myself.

After a few eons, my lawyer came out and said they were dropping the case.

"Hallelujah!" But there was a catch: I had to plead guilty to a non-criminal violation.

"No way."

"They need to cover their ass, so they want you to plead to something."

"What kind of violation?"

"Like a traffic ticket."

"No way. Tell them this is a bunch of bullshit. I want a trial."

"They're also willing to seal the court records and totally dismiss the case after a year. It would be like it never happened."

"I don't know."

"Look, this thing will be over. No trial and it will be dropped in 12 months. You'll be home free."

"So they drum up two felony charges, ruin my career and are willing to drop the whole thing if I plead to a violation?"

"There's one more thing. You have to pay back the youth league seven hundred and fifty bucks for the letter they sent out."

"Are you kidding?"

"That's the deal. You should take it."

"What about all the bullshit they put me through?"

"There's not much we can do about that."

"Can I sue the bastards?"

"Not likely. You were indicted by a grand jury, not the DA, and you can't sue them."

It would certainly be an end to a long, hard road of shit I wouldn't wish on anyone. I thought of the poor kid next door.

"If it will close the case and stop the press releases, I'll do it."

A few people had wandered over who couldn't get in next door and the judge cleared them out of the courtroom. In exchange for dropping the two felony charges, I pled guilty to one count of criminal solicitation in the sixth degree—it took them a good hour in the back room to come up with that one—with the proviso that the records would be sealed and the violation dismissed as long as I didn't get in trouble during the next 12 months. I left them with a check for the league.

Back outside, the samurai circus had cleared out and the corridor was empty. The assistant DA came up to me. "I'm sorry about all of this," he said. "I was just doing my job."

For the first time in a long time I was speechless.

The Mayor of West Meadow responded with a letter to the editor:

Now that the criminal charges have been dropped against former Brookhaven Parks Commissioner Bob Chartuk, it's time to say a few words about a man whose reputation has been unfairly attacked and whose many accomplishments swept under the rug.

As a retired public school counselor and administrator I focused some of my attention over the last few years on our local government, particularly the condition of our parks system. Projects never got off the drawing board, department morale was extremely low, and several of the most basic of repairs were never accomplished.

When I went looking for answers, Commissioner Chartuk was one of a few at town hall who found the time to meet with me and start turning things around. Bob showed up with a clipboard and took notes. He had that rare quality that I respect from our elected officials—He listened to what I had to say and shared my vision of how the town's parks should be.

After years of neglect, he made one of my favorite parks, West Meadow Beach, a priority and soon, the buildings were painted, bathrooms fixed, roofs repaired, and the sand piles, litter, and weeds in the parking lot removed. He saw to it that the rusted fences were replaced, sprinklers in the kiddie park fixed, benches and picnic tables cleaned and the parking lot repaired. We had hot water in the bathrooms for the first time in years. He took my suggestion on how to stop people from speeding through the parking lot and installed speed bumps. He even had the pulley fixed on the flagpole so we could finally raise the red, white, and blue.

Spending time with Commissioner Chartuk, we experienced what it takes to get something done in a bureaucracy and I saw firsthand how much effort, skill, and integrity he put into the job. His results over four years were outstanding. He created a union-management partnership that put needed equipment, materials, and tools in the hands of the parks employees and they responded by dramatically increasing production. Morale turned around and the staff took great pride in their work. He used town employees, instead of expensive contractors, to do much of the work in building the 18-acre Heritage Park in Mt. Sinai, a project that would cost ten times the amount if attempted today.

He managed the renovation of Davis Park and the Pine Neck Marina and Sand Spit Park in Patchogue. Great Gun Beach saw major improvements under Commissioner Chartuk and he built new ball fields with a new bathroom, irrigation, and parking lot at Sipp Avenue in Medford and also built new fields and parking with Community Development funds at Martha Avenue in Bellport. He renovated the historic Swan River School House in East Patchogue and the Acampora Recreation Center in Blue Point. He cleaned up Miramar Beach in East Patchogue and made sure maintenance was kept up at all of our parks and playgrounds.

He built new parks at Pine Lake in Middle Island and Osprey Park in Mastic Beach and practically re-constructed the entire Mt. Sinai Marina, three environmental restoration projects that dramatically improved water quality. He was a commissioner that led massive environmental cleanups removing tons of garbage and debris from the town's open space holdings such as Grove Street in Patchogue and the Orchard Neck Preserve in Center Moriches and dredged the muck out of Senix Creek, not to mention a complete refurbishment of Neville Park in Center Moriches after decades of decay.

He focused much-needed attention on the Longwood Estate, the town's historic cemeteries, Lake Grove Church, and even the Firemen's Memorial Park in Ridge which showed off its improvements by hosting one of the best fire tournaments in state history.

Across the town, parking lots were repaired, playgrounds renovated, and fencing at parks and ball fields replaced. He re-wrote service contracts and procurement specs for everything from plumbing supplies to grass seed saving the taxpayers thousands of dollars.

Above all, he was a family man who proudly brought his wife and daughters to park grand openings and town events. I'll never forget seeing him working alongside parks employees planting beach grass and trees and picking up litter. Due to his fairness and work ethic, he earned their respect and support and they in turn worked hard for him and the taxpayers.

The list of Bob Chartuk's accomplishments goes on for many pages and I challenge any municipality on Long Island to match it. The District Attorney did a good job weeding out corruption in town government, but with Commissioner Chartuk, he went too far and I'm glad his case was discharged. To paraphrase a famous quote: Where does he go now to get his reputation back?

CHAPTER 75

UNSTOPPABLE

True to his word, John appeared on Oprah, a special live broadcast, to announce his run for the White House. The talk show host was ecstatic, as was her studio audience who would have swooned the entire hour if John didn't politely quiet them down. America was listening too and "Kennedy Mania" as the New York Times dubbed it, took hold of the nation. Goldstone booked the Keefe Auditorium in Nashua for John's first New Hampshire visit and even the state's largest performing arts center wasn't big enough to contain the enthusiasm. The scene was repeated in Iowa and the higher John soared, the lower the Four Black Men sank. Hillary Clinton signed on as secretary of state and appeared with John in Obama's home state where the Kennedy juggernaut maxed out Cellular Field and, not to exclude White Sox fans, repeated the feat at Wrigley.

The Four Black Men threw a Hail Mary.

"We can get Obama to drop out in exchange for Vice President and some considerations for us."

John ignored them and was a week away from wrapping up the delegates he would need for the Democrat nomination.

"This is exciting," Sandra said at the bar. "He's actually doing it."

"No doubt in my mind he'd be the president if he were alive," Harvard chimed in.

"No doubt about it," echoed Big Daddy.

"You see," Sandra turned to me, "you set things right. For all your doom and gloom and stories about fate and death and what's wrong with the freaking world, you took care of John."

The bar nodded in agreement and Sandra reveled in the moment. "You saved him from crashing his plane and made him a hero. You made him a senator and even gave us a baby, little John the Third. Now he's going to be the president. I'm glad I ran into you."

CHAPTER 76

FOLEY'S FOLLY

In a lame attempt to show that the case had nothing to with politics, the DA waited until the day after Brian Foley's election as town supervisor to arrest me. His campaign to besmirch the Republicans had worked its magic and Foley won. Since I had only been suspended as commissioner, one of his first official acts was to fire me with great fanfare. Ironically, it was the Democrat-created ward system that saved the Republicans. Had the candidates run at large with Foley, the Dems probably would have won every seat. But the ward system shoe was on the other foot and three Republicans were able to win their districts.

As a tribute to Brian Foley's great management skills, work at Neville Park stopped the week he took office and didn't start again until eight months later. Still, he took every opportunity to bad mouth the parks department, telling anyone who'd listen it was so mismanaged that nobody could even tell him where all the parks were. I was tempted to call the papers to say that all Foley had to do was roll out the 10-foot list in my office, but didn't bother.

Foley did such a bang up job in Brookhaven they ran him for the state senate three years later. Mostly because the Republicans wanted to get him out of town hall, he won, and became the first Democratic senator elected from Suffolk since 1902. Foley's victory put his party in charge of both houses of the legislature for the first time since 1965 and the state's power base shifted to New York City. Instantly, the assault on suburbia began. Cow-towing to his Democrat masters, Foley cast the deciding vote for a new payroll tax that funneled billions of dollars from Long Island to the New York City subways. The scheme was particularly onerous because local governments like the town were also forced to pay it which amounted to double taxation without, thanks to Foley, representation. His vote was the last one needed to slash school funding and he cast the deciding vote to eliminate the STAR property tax rebate checks the Republicans had delivered for Long Island year after year. The first state budget he voted on increased spending by $16 billion with hardly any of it going to his home district. His vote cranked up motor vehicle fees and business taxes and, adding insult to injury, he even figured out how to tax one of the last things people around here get to do for free by imposing a salt water fishing license. Senator Foley was a disaster and cost Long Island billions. If there ever was someone guilty of official misconduct it was him. Thankfully, the voters booted him out after only one term.

Shortly after his ignominious defeat, I ran into him on the Long Island Rail Road heading home from Penn Station. It was the last leg of a trip he made to Albany to call in favors for a political job so he could keep his state pension clock ticking. Given how much money he transferred from the people to the politicians, they should have rolled out a red carpet. The train was packed and I had a seat. Foley didn't and had to stand by the doors like a commoner. I asked the lady next to me to save my place and I went over to have a few words with Mr. Foley.

"So, Brian, how are you?"

"I'm fine and you?"

"Pretty good after you fired me."

"Well, that's just something we had to do."

"What are you up to now?"

"Heading back from Albany."

"Looking for a new job, huh?"

"Just meeting people up there."

"You should have a few chips to cash in with the Albany crowd after the votes you took."

"Not really," he said, looking pretty fidgety.

"What were you thinking when you passed the payroll tax? I mean Long Island has to pay billions for the New York subways. How fair is that?"

"It was a regional issue, something that needed to be done," he explained as the train wheels clicked below. It was going to be a long ride.

"How come you did away with the tax rebate checks?" I asked next. "Long Island pays the highest taxes in the nation and you took away their only relief. That's nuts."

"The state just couldn't afford it."

"Well, the taxpayers got their revenge. What did you lose the election by, 20 percent?"

No answer.

"Anyhow, that salt water fishing license was the craziest thing I ever heard. Whatever convinced you to do that?"

"It's a complicated issue."

"I have all day."

"I'd rather not get into it," he replied, staring at the floor.

"You increased motor vehicle fees, business taxes, cut school funding. Boy, I hope they give you a great job."

No answer.

And what about Neville Park? The job stopped cold the day you took office."

Without looking at me, Foley tucked his newspaper under his arm and started off down the aisle.

"One more thing, Brian." He looked back.

"The parks. The location of all the parks."

"What about them?"

"All you had to do was look in my office. There was a list 10 feet long."

The only empty seat in the car was the one the lady was holding for me and he went to take it.

"Sorry, saved," she told him as I cut in and sat down.

He went back by the doors and buried his head in the paper. If the working stiffs on that train knew how bad Brian Foley screwed them, he wouldn't have made it home.

CHAPTER 77

THE END

John John's friends were the first to pick up on it and then his staff and associates realized it too: the Senator had never shaken the cough he picked up at Ground Zero and with each passing day his voice grew more and more raspy. His youthful appearance and vigor was leaving him. He hated that Carolyn had to hear his coughing and had taken to going into the hallway for the worst of the outbursts, his red face and watery eyes giving him away.

A week before the Democratic National Convention in Denver where his coronation for president was set to occur, Senator Kennedy took to the airways in a hastily called news conference. He had won every state in his primary campaign against Barack Obama and was favored to crush Senator John McCain, the Republican. The nation was on the edge of its seat wondering what the America icon planned to tell them on such short notice.

"I have contracted pulmonary fibrosis, a disease of the lungs, from my time at Ground Zero in Manhattan," John pulled no punches. "I regretfully announce that I am not fit to run for president at this time."

The nation went into shock.

"Therefore, I am pledging my convention delegates to Senator Obama who has my full support and endorsement to be the next president of the United States."

Six months later, on the eve of the inauguration of the president, John F. Kennedy, Jr. passed away with his family and friends at his bedside.

POSTSCRIPT

The National Weather Service got all of its new weather stations up and running and I'd like to think that I made some small contribution to a program that saves lives.

Sometimes I think about John John and Danny, Mugsy and the Monarch and the wildly different directions of their lives. I pain over those who were worthy and are gone and those who are very much alive and suffering in their self-created hell. If God is testing them, they will get their just reward.

I bring my daughter to the playground they built in memory of Flight 800 not far from Deadman's Curve and the little gingerbread house where I grew up. There's a pink granite monument at the park's entrance engraved with the names of the victims and she would always leapfrog over it. When she gets older, I'll tell her the stories of her home town and when I do I'll mention the eerie gold and silver that lit up the ocean that night—a shipment of glitter that was in the cargo hold of Flight 800.

Sometimes we'll hear a noisy plane overhead with a glider attached by a long, thin line. It's Gruff and his tow pilot still taking people up to find their dreams.

It was a summer day that saw the end of the dreams of Kennworth Eaton, the pilot who took me north. He disappeared from radar on approach to Gabreski Airport and was never seen again. Months later, I found a piece of an engine on the beach. Whether it was from his plane, I do not know.

Printed in the United States
By Bookmasters